Politics & Symbols

Politics & Symbols

The Italian Communist Party and
the Fall of Communism

David I. Kertzer

Yale University Press   New Haven and London

Designed by Sonia L. Scanlon.
Set in Minion type by Jennifer Kaufman DTP.
Printed in the United States of America by BookCrafters, Inc., Chelsea, Michigan.

Library of Congress Cataloging-in-Publication Data

Kertzer, David I., 1948–
Politics and symbols : the Italian Communist Party and the fall
of communism / David I. Kertzer.
p.   cm.
Includes bibliographical references and index.
ISBN 0-300-06612-0 (cloth: alk. paper)
0-300-07724-6 (pbk.: alk. paper)
1. Partito comunista italiano.   2. Partito democratico della
sinistra.   3. Symbolism in politics—Italy.   I. Title.
JN5657.C63K47   1996
324.245'075—dc20   95-47703
CIP

A catalogue record for this book is available from the British Library.

The paper in this book meets the guidelines for permanence and durability
of the Committee on Production Guidelines for Book Longevity of the Council on
Library Resources.

10   9   8   7   6   5   4   3   2

For Bernardo Bernardi

amico prezioso

contents

preface

In 1971–72, as a graduate student doing fieldwork for my doctoral dissertation, I spent a year in a working-class *quartiere* of Bologna, at the center of Italy's "red belt." I found there a world I had never seen, one in which the Italian Communist Party (Partito comunista italiano, or PCI) occupied the center not only of political life but of social and intellectual life as well. Attending weekly meetings of the local party sections, frequenting the cafés where party members and sympathizers gathered daily, and participating in a wide range of other activities—from rallies and protest marches to neighborhood Communist *feste*—I gradually grew to understand and appreciate the role played by the PCI in the lives of its members, at least in this heavily Communist zone.

In the next two and a half decades, I returned frequently to Italy and to Bologna. Although I often traveled there for quite different purposes, my attention always returned to the PCI and the people associated with it. In these years, back in my old quartiere, I saw most of the old guard—those who had joined the party in the tumultuous transitional years between war and peace, Fascism and the new republic—gradually die off. Of the once young party activists I knew, a few gradually drifted away from politics, but most remained, and some even rose through the party hierarchy to attain full-time political positions.

In spite of all the time I have subsequently spent in Italy, the images of the PCI that remain most vivid for me are the memories of my first year in Bologna, when somehow people welcomed me, taking my wife, Susan, and me in and educating us in the ways of the quartiere and the ways of the party. It was a time when the Vietnam War was on everyone's mind, and as an American eager to speak out against the war I was a welcome addition to an assortment of party-sponsored demonstrations and rallies. It was a time when people, young and old, would happily sit around a dinner table singing songs of the Resistance and songs of the old peasant leagues of the turn of the century. It was a time when, Sunday after Sunday, every doorbell was rung by a comrade selling *L'Unità*, the party paper, when those who identified themselves as Catholics refused to play tennis on (public) courts identified as Communist, and when many Communists preferred burial by comrades—holding their red flags aloft—to a funeral presided over by a priest.

Even before the main events with which this book is concerned—the abandonment by the Communist Party of its Communist identity in 1989–91—occurred, the level of popular participation in party activities, and the extent to which people identified with the party, had declined. Indeed, in some ways it was a crisis in this form of party identification, in this level of involvement, in the permeation by the PCI of local social life, that would lead to the dramatic events that I describe in the pages ahead.

This is a book that I hope will prove to be provocative, though I know that my perspective is one that not all readers are likely to find to their taste. It is a book about national politics that is written not by a political scientist but from the perspective of an anthropologist. Many matters that would be featured in more standard political accounts are given only cursory attention here, and many matters that I find most significant and worth pursuing most fully are likely to be regarded as of only secondary concern by other political analysts.

The claim of this book is that politics depends heavily—indeed integrally—on symbolism, and that symbolic change has important political and material consequences. If the case I make in these pages does not convince everyone, I hope at least that the book will force readers to engage the argument and reflect deeply on the view of politics presented here.

I have many people to thank for educating me about Italian politics in general and the PCI in particular, from those earliest conversations, long into the night, in Bolognese bars and party section headquarters a quarter century ago to those today conducted through cyberspace. I would especially like to express gratitude to Arturo Parisi, inexhaustible font of political wisdom. Many of the ideas developed in this book took shape through long conversations with Arturo, although I am not sure he will always recognize them. I would also like to thank Arturo's colleagues at the Istituto Cattaneo in Bologna, which has long provided me with a scholarly home away from home.

Research support for this work was provided by funds connected to the William Kenan Professorship at Bowdoin College and the Paul Dupee, Jr., University Professorship at Brown University.

The work also depended on the goodwill of officials in the Italian Communist Party, who unfailingly welcomed my research forays, from inviting me to national party congresses to facilitating my access to party documents and materials. Unless otherwise noted, all translations are my own.

I benefited greatly from comments on an earlier draft of this book by Stephen Hellman and Jane Schneider. I would like to pay special tribute to Steve, whose many challenging questions about the draft led me to rethink a number of issues and produced a better book (although one in which I am sure he will still see much to disagree with). Thanks also to my students, Frank Biess and Arnaldo Ferroni, for their comments on the manuscript. Finally, I would like to thank Charles Grench and Tina Weiner of Yale University Press for their support of this project, and Jenya Weinreb for her deft editing of the manuscript.

chapter one

Naming Names

Stretching out into the periphery of Bologna, behind the train station, just beyond the old walls of the city, lies the *quartiere* of Bolognina (little Bologna). In a city that symbolized Italian Communism, a city ruled by a Communist mayor since the fall of Fascism, Bolognina was Communism's popular epicenter. In this quartiere of working-class families, Communism was as much a part of people's identities as their pride in the cuisine for which they were famous. Indeed, critics charged, Communism was these people's religion, a faith, complete with complex liturgy and holy hierarchy. When asked, "Are you a Catholic?" a citizen of Bolognina was likely to reply, "No, I'm Communist."

If Communism was the religion of the people of Bolognina, there was no more sacred memory than that of the time when Nazi troops occupied Bologna, aided by their Italian quislings in Mussolini's puppet government, the Republic of Salò. Salvation, in this drama, came not from divine intervention but from the heroic deeds of the Communist people of Bologna. Lightly armed and surrounded by Nazi forces, the Communist-inspired partisans took on the ruthless Nazi killing machine. Through their martyrdom, not only Bologna but all Italy was delivered from evil, and the modern, democratic era was ushered in.

To nourish the memory of these sacred events, the people of Bologna developed an elaborate ritual calendar to recall the *Resistenza*—as this patchwork of anti-Nazi activities came to be called. Not only was time divided into sacred periods in this way but space was as well, for certain places were made into shrines or pilgrimage sites. In Bologna, the holiest of such dates came in

November. On November 7, 1944, partisan forces descended on Porta Lame, the gate to the central city near the train station, and a violent battle ensued, leaving, it was said, 216 Fascists dead but only 12 partisan casualties. Fighting erupted again a week later, in the midst of Bolognina, leaving more Resistance martyrs behind. According to popular belief, 17 *partigiani* at Bolognina had taken on 900 Fascists and Nazis who were supported by tanks and armored cars. It would be another five months before the Nazis were driven out of the city, when Allied troops marched in to delirious popular celebration.

To mark the battle of Bolognina, as the episode came to be called, the association of partisans, fighters in the Liberation struggle, each year held a commemorative ceremony. In the early postwar years these generated a good deal of popular participation, but by the late 1980s, aside from various local political officials—mainly Communist—participants consisted primarily of the aging partigiani themselves, dressed in their best suits and ties and donning their special partisan hats for the march through the streets of the quartiere, proudly holding aloft the banners emblazoned with the names of their battalions.

Nothing had prepared the partigiani assembled at Bolognina's civic center for what greeted them as they waited for ceremonies to begin on November 11, 1989. Just as the forty-fifth anniversary ceremonies were about to begin, in strode Achille Occhetto, national head of the Italian Communist Party, heir to the legendary Antonio Gramsci, Palmiro Togliatti, and Enrico Berlinguer. The excitement was palpable, the pleasure immense.

But what might have been simply another symbolic reinforcement of the ties binding the party periphery to its center was to become much more. As a result of Occhetto's visit, Bolognina would, ironically, become a symbol of the end of the PCI, the demise of not only a political party but a personal identity that gave special meaning to the lives of most of the elderly partisans assembled in that Bolognina hall.

Occhetto began his brief talk by paying homage to the Bolognina martyrs and, to the delight of his listeners, stressing the importance of transmitting the "values of the national Liberation struggle" to the younger generations. This, he argued, was particularly important in light of recent events in Eastern Europe. Indeed, the Berlin Wall had just begun to be torn down, and Occhetto used the Resistance to distance the PCI from the East German Communists. "The building of this wall was not in the spirit of the Resistance," the party secretary proclaimed.

Occhetto compared his address at Bolognina to Mikhail Gorbachev's earlier appearance before a group of World War II veterans. It was at that appearance that Gorbachev announced the need for perestroika: "You won the Second World War," Occhetto quoted his Soviet counterpart as saying, "if you don't want it all lost now we must not cling to the past but devote ourselves to making great changes." Given the dizzying pace of political events in 1989, Occhetto added, "we must move ahead with the same courage that was then demonstrated in the Resistance."

As Occhetto prepared to join those assembled for the procession to place a wreath at the monument to the martyrs of the battle of Bolognina, he was stopped by a journalist, who asked whether his remarks hinted at a plan to change the name of the Communist Party. The PCI secretary replied, "They hint at everything . . . we are undertaking great changes and innovations in all directions." With this offhanded comment, in the modest quartiere headquarters of Bolognina, a political storm began that would not only alter the political future of Italy but also trigger a deeply wrenching personal drama for hundreds of thousands of Italians, Communists shorn of their identity, clinging uneasily to tarnished symbols.[1]

The Symbolic Bases of Politics

For many political analysts, there is the "real" stuff of politics and then there are the effluvia of political life: symbols, ceremonies, flag-waving, and baby-kissing. In this view, those observers who are sophisticated enough to peer through the surface, littered as it is with various sops to the credulous, are able to see that what explains political action are such hard-nosed matters as financial interest and the jostling for personal gain, the grim workings, in short, of rational choice.

In this book I contest these widely held views. In doing so, I tell two tales. The first, whose preamble led off this chapter, is the tale of the transformation of the largest Communist Party ever found in a country where the CP was not in power. It is a story of political trauma, of dramatic showdowns in the limelight and personal dramas far from public view. It tells of the struggle to change, practically overnight, a political identity that was constructed and reconstructed over many decades. It tells, in short, of one of the more notable episodes in the worldwide political drama of 1989–91, when Communist parties were not only rejected but disgraced.

My second tale, interwoven with the first, is that of politics itself. I use the case of the besieged Italian Communists to ask what role symbolism plays in modern politics, how important it is and why, how it works and how it fails.

At its root, politics is symbolic, because both the formation of human groupings and the hierarchies that spring from them depend on symbolic activity. What makes me an American, what gives me the notion that I live in Rhode Island, what leads me to think of myself as a Democrat or a Republican, a conservative or a revolutionary? Clearly none of these political identities are based on objects I can touch or see or perceive in any way except through symbolic representation.

Now some might object that much of politics involves not symbolism but simply relations of force—at its extreme, brute physical power. And it is true that an Iraqi drafted into Saddam Hussein's army might join regardless of any symbolic construction he places on his duties as an Iraqi, or that a person tempted to take someone else's property might think twice simply for fear of arrest. Yet these sorts of power to constrain are not simply, or even essentially, a physical power, for they presuppose a symbolic power. The power of the government to compel a person to act in certain ways is based on its ability to mobilize people to do its bidding. This in turn inevitably depends on symbolic activity: identifying who citizens are, what their duties to the government are, and just who represents "government" in the first place. Even property and ownership are essentially symbolic processes: material goods and rights to services can be assigned to individuals only through symbolism.

Pierre Bourdieu has written of this process in terms of "political capital," a form of the broader category of "symbolic capital." In his formulation, political capital "exists only in and through representation. . . . It is a power which exists because the person who submits to it believes that it exists."

Two questions are basic to any understanding of how politics works, how authority is established, and how power is wielded: (1) how are the symbols underlying political life constructed and altered? and (2) by what process do people come to recognize certain symbols as legitimate and others as illegitimate? Bourdieu tells us that the political leader "derives his truly magical power over the group from faith in the representation that he gives to the group." But how do people come to endow their leaders' representations with their faith?[2]

These two issues come into sharp focus in the case of one particularly important sort of symbolic innovation: the act of naming. Naming was central to the crisis suffered by the Italian Communist Party in 1989–91—for nothing generated more anguish than the proposal that the Communist name be dropped. Yet the problem of the name has hardly made its way to the radar screen of political study; in the dominant view of political power relations, it is viewed as a sideshow, of little consequence. Curiously, in the case of the PCI, the contenders for power in the party leadership themselves took up the question—previously more typically posed by philosophers than politicians—of the relation between the name and the "thing."

Another way of putting this is simply, do names matter in politics and, if so, what does this tell us about what politics is all about? The problem of the name, then, permeates both tales in this book. Political representation ultimately comes down to the ways in which individuals are assigned, or assign themselves, to political groups. How do we come to identify ourselves with people we do not know, in opposition to others we will never see? Politics in large-scale societies is based on just this process of group identity.

Symbols play a crucial role in relating one group to another. By both promoting a certain view of the world and stirring up emotion, symbols impel people to action. "The more antagonistic a social situation," the Polish anthropologist Zdzislaw Mach writes, "the more active role symbolic actions play, integrating a group, canalizing conflicts or, often, generating open action against opponents or enemies." In the place of the morass of potentially an infinity of possible ways of dividing people into categories and hence placing them in the same category as ourselves or outside it, such symbols "polarize the world, enhance oppositions between partners, and define them in clear terms ideologically patterned and saturated with emotions."[3]

Symbols are politically important not only in regulating group identity but in providing people with their own personal identities as well. Let me begin with an example. Not long ago, in Perugia, an elderly man died. Although he undoubtedly had been baptized, his funeral was not held in church. Rather, his friends, neighbors, and family joined in a Communist funeral. Laid out in the battle dress that identified him as a veteran of the Garibaldi brigade, a fighter in the Resistance, he clutched a red handkerchief. As visitors arrived to pay their respects, they heard the stirring sounds of the "Internationale." The music came from a tape recorder nestled beside the corpse's head.[4]

For the former partisan, current identity—even posthumous identity—was tied to a world of symbolism that linked him both to larger political entities—the Italian Communist Party and the Communist movement worldwide—and to a particular construction of the past and his relation to it. We all fashion identities for ourselves; we tell stories about ourselves to ourselves as well as to others. Threats to such symbolic constructions represent threats to our most basic selves.

The symbols by which we define ourselves in the present, and the symbols by which we identify with larger political groupings and make sense of the political world around us, are for the most part symbols that represent the past. The past, like the present, otherwise presents itself to us as totally chaotic; we need to make it graspable, to reduce it to a few comprehensible themes, if we are to find a place for ourselves in it.

In *The Past Is a Foreign Country,* David Lowenthal argued that we need a stable past "to confirm our own identity, and to make sense of the present." Yet in situations of political change, such as that faced by Communists throughout the world in 1989, the nature of the past is contested, and with it people's identity in the present is challenged. Changing the past threatens to undermine our construction of ourselves, while pressures to change our political identity in the present press us to rewrite the past, that is, to alter the symbolic construction of the past.

The debate over the uses of the past has many strands and a long tradition. Perhaps the most uncomfortable question for historians is the extent to which historians themselves are engaged in the constant remaking of the past to suit current political interests (a theme I will take up in Chapter 5). Michel Foucault, who is often cited in this context, maintains that what we remember about the past is a matter of how the past is represented, and that such representations are produced by those who hold power in the present.[5]

The battle in the Italian Communist Party in the wake of the fall of the Berlin Wall (a nice metaphorical as well as material construction) was fought in good part over the terrain of history. Successfully changing current political identity meant successfully reconstructing the past. Likewise, efforts to block such change entailed the tenacious defense of the past.

Some historians might object that what I am talking about here is not history but myth, that is, not an objective account of the past but a sacred tale. As I will explain in Chapter 5, I see problems in any simple division between history, the clear-eyed product of professional historians, and myth, the fuzzy product of the historically uninformed. I do think, however, that much more serious attention needs to be given to the role of myth in modern politics. In Bronislaw Malinowski's classic formulation, myth (which he nevertheless identified with the "savage community") "is not merely a story told but a reality lived." He called it a "narrative resurrection of a primeval reality," which fulfills indispensable functions: expressing, enhancing, and codifying belief, safeguarding and enforcing morality, vouching for the efficiency of ritual, and providing "practical rules for the guidance of man."[6]

Although my focus is on the use of myth by the Italian Communist Party, my intent is not to argue that the Communists were unusual in their dependence on myth. Quite the contrary: all modern political parties rely on myth, and parallel studies of political mythology could profitably be done in Italy on parties from the Right and the Center as well.[7]

For the Italian Communists these sacred tales—tales of the October Revolution, the heroic Resistance, the battle of the working class against capitalism and imperialism—underlay not only their identity but also their sense that they were the chosen people. It was they who were at the vanguard of history.[8]

I thus challenge the notion that politics can be understood primarily in terms of rational actors behaving according to a stable set of interests. The challenge stems from two observations: (1) that political perceptions and hence the definition of the political situation are themselves necessarily symbolically constructed; and (2) that people are as driven by emotion as they are by any dispassionate calculation of personal interest.

My position, although at odds with some influential approaches in political science and political sociology, is in keeping with major traditions in cultural anthropology and political psychology. Psychologist David Sears, for example, contrasted a "symbolic politics" approach with one based on rational choice. In the symbolic politics view, individuals do not cognitively assess "current information in a realistic, sensible manner." Rather, people are resistant to change. "Symbolic processing may," writes Sears, "ultimately serve rational ends for the individual or for the society, but if it does, it is not through a process of careful and rational deliberation or cost-benefit analysis." Indeed, he concludes, the "best evidence is that self-interest has relatively little impact on political attitudes."[9] I would add only that self-interest itself is not a given, determinable a priori by an outside judge, but rather a cultural product, based on a symbolic process.

A focus on the importance of symbolism in politics and political change has likewise enjoyed a good deal of popularity among historians since the mid-1980s. Indeed, this period has seen a boom in studies by historians that focus on political symbolism and the staging of political ritual.

Nowhere has the impact of this historiographical movement been greater than in France. The study of politics in French history—as in most other national histories—had previously consisted of inquiries into great personages, military engagements, and the development of ideologies and institutions. Yet a sharp shift occurred in the 1980s, referred to by Patrick Hutton as a move "from the history of politics to the politics of culture," an approach that offers a "methodological alternative to the history of ideas."[10]

One of the most influential historians in this movement in the United States has been George Mosse. In his view, political ideas are formulated and transmitted not through rational calculations but, rather, through a symbolic process. Although unwilling to jettison the Enlightenment belief in an objective, fixed reality, Mosse argues that people can perceive this reality only through the myths and symbols that guide their perception.[11]

Mosse and other historians of his generation were strongly influenced by the experience of Nazism. The mass hysteria that swept up the German people, a people previously viewed as at the vanguard of modern, rational, Western society, led many historians and political philosophers to stress the irrational element of political life. Yet in doing so they tried to hold on to an image of history and social analysis that depended on the assumption of a fixed reality.

I don't doubt that some things are real—to take a sadly relevant example, that millions of Jews died at the hands of Nazis and their followers during the war. Yet even such glimpses of reality, insofar as we can get at them, must be conceptualized and communicated in our own symbolic terms. These are themselves linked to symbolic constructions that had meaning for the people of the past (such terms as *Jew* and *Nazi*) and to those that emerged only later (such terms as *Holocaust*).

If we reflect a bit on this link, the clear distinction between the history of the historian and the history of the uneducated becomes uncomfortably blurred. Or, at least, we lose the certainty that while others see the past through a symbolic lens, we somehow see it directly, as it was. I do not mean that all versions of history are equal, that there can be no basis for judging one more accurate than another, or that questions of evidence are irrelevant. I mean only that there is no way we can deal with the past without imposing symbolic constructions on it.

Becoming Post-Communist

Achille Occhetto's comments at Bolognina, and his subsequent announced intention to change the name of the Italian Communist Party and to give birth to a "new political formation," came as a bombshell to party members. The subject of casting off the Communist name and identity had hitherto been taboo. No PCI leader had publicly broached the possibility, although the subject periodically came up when others suggested that such a repudiation was necessary to demonstrate the party's break with its Soviet-influenced past.[12] Indeed, what came to be known as the "K factor" in Italian politics—the pall cast over the PCI by its international Communist affiliation—continued to be cited by political observers as grounds for the continued exclusion of the PCI from participation in coalition governments.[13] The "K factor" persisted even though for decades the PCI had been progressively moving away from its pro-Soviet stance and away from much of what traditionally defined the Communist ideology of the party.

Occhetto had consulted very few others in the party leadership before announcing what came to be known as the *svolta,* or turnabout. As party leader since 1988, he well knew the difficulties of placating the various party factions, and recognized the obstacles he faced in effecting change. The party had long contended with divisions between Right and Left, although these had for the most part been kept in check by the practice of democratic centralism, a ban on any formal factional activity, and a disinclination to voice public criticism of the party line. This Leninist tradition of democratic centralism had slowly eroded over the years—a process that accelerated in the mid-1980s—yet its legacy lingered.

In deciding on the svolta, Occhetto was motivated in good part by strategic considerations involving other Italian political forces. By the late 1980s the PCI found itself without any credible alliance strategy that could bring it into the national government. The party was prevented from a broad leftist alliance strategy by the position taken by the Socialist Party and its powerful leader, Bettino Craxi. Craxi, who would suffer a spectacular fall from power just a few years later, also blocked the PCI's efforts to join the Socialist International and its efforts to join the Socialist Party group in the European parliament. In this context, no credible alliance plan for displacing the Christian Democrats was available, and, with the simultaneous collapse of the Communist regimes in Eastern Europe, the PCI, in Michele Salvati's words, "was declining and heading towards a dead end."[14]

Those on the party's Left, however, saw the matter differently. Pietro Ingrao, the most prominent exponent of this camp, argued that the reason for the PCI's declining fortunes in the 1980s was its failure to articulate a clear and vigorous anti-capitalist, pro-worker position. In other words, for Ingrao the problem was the party's movement away from its Marxist roots.

Also on the party's Left was the smaller, philo-Soviet faction led by Armando Cossutta. Cossutta and those of like mind were unhappy about the way the PCI had progressively distanced itself from the Soviet Union and from the Communist Parties of Eastern Europe. The world's problems, for them, could be simply laid at the feet of worldwide capitalism and American imperialism.

Giorgio Napolitano long incarnated what was known as the right, or reformist, wing of the PCI. According to the reformists, the PCI's Communist rhetoric was both outmoded and counterproductive in attracting the support the party needed in an increasingly wealthy society. This reform wing of the party identified with the social democratic parties of Europe (especially the German Sozialdemokratische Partei Deutschlands [SPD] and the British Labour Party) and saw the PCI's future niche as that of providing a similar reformist party for Italy.[15]

Occhetto—and his predecessors as party secretary over the previous two decades—uneasily straddled the party Center, sometimes allied with one wing and sometimes with the other. In contemplating the purging of the party's Communist identity, Occhetto could be confident of the support of the reformist wing. The challenge was to attract solid support from the Center and hope that, when confronted with the resulting majority, the left wing of the party would recognize the impossibility of victory and come to terms with the change.

It was in this fractious context that Occhetto announced to the press, in the days following his Bolognina visit, that he was proposing a plan to transform the PCI into something else, a new force that would appeal to a much broader segment of progressive opinion in

Italy. The goal was to build a political grouping capable of attracting sufficient electoral support to displace the Christian Democrats, who had ruled the country uninterrupted for the previous forty years. The process of transformation would involve a *fase costituente*, a constituent phase, in which the nature of the new political entity (he did not yet refer to it as a party) would be crafted.[16]

At the end of November, just a couple of weeks after Occhetto first announced his intentions, a dramatic meeting of the party's Central Committee was held in Rome. Speaker after speaker got up, some to praise and others to condemn the move. Occhetto came away with a solid majority: two-thirds of the members voted in his favor. Yet this result must be put in the proper context. A one-third vote against a party secretary was unprecedented in PCI history; in the past, votes had typically been unanimous.

Ultimate approval of the proposal would require the holding of a special, "extraordinary" national party congress. This was to involve much more than the four-day national congress itself, for the party's statutes required that members to such a congress be elected via a capillary process beginning with special congresses of each of the thousands of local party sections that dotted the country. At each of these, the proposed platform was voted on, and delegates were elected to the next higher level, ultimately leading to the election of eleven hundred delegates to the national congress.

Unlike any national party congress since the war's end, the special congress of 1990 had before it not simply the secretary's proposal but two opposing proposals as well, so that the delegates had to choose from among three competing plans. In the three months leading up to the national congress, which was held in Bologna in March 1990, each faction campaigned vigorously.

Motion 1, drafted by Occhetto, called for the party's transformation into a "new political formation." It aimed to enlarge the traditional base of the Communist Party, by appealing to a wide array of progressive movements. Motion 2 was backed not only by Ingrao and his supporters on the Left but also by a number of the most prominent leaders of the party Center, including the previous party secretary, Alessandro Natta. It condemned Occhetto's initiative, ridiculing it as vague and poorly conceived, and spoke of the traditional Communist identity and symbolism as a matter of great pride and value. Motion 3, identified with Cossutta and the extreme Left of the party, likewise opposed Occhetto's proposal and argued that with the end of the Cold War and the constraining effect that it had had on Italian politics, a bright future lay ahead for the Italian Communist Party.

Occhetto ended up reproducing his two-thirds majority at the Bologna congress (the PCI's nineteenth) and winning re-election as party secretary by a similar margin.[17] He hoped that, with this approval of the entire party via the Nineteenth Party Congress, the battle over abandoning the old party identity would be behind him. This, however, was not to be. Yet another national congress—the twentieth and, as it turned out, last PCI congress—would have to be held to formalize the foundation of a new party. Because the PCI was still in existence, leaders of the opposition argued, and because the twentieth congress would be a sovereign decision-making body of the PCI, the new congress had the prerogative of rejecting the course on which Occhetto had recklessly set out.

The months following the nineteenth congress were marked by acrimonious internal party debates and mutual denunciations similar to those that had characterized the brief period leading up to the congress. Rather than join forces with Occhetto, the minority, committed to retaining the party's Communist identity, sought to build a new majority to defeat him.

The crisis in the party provoked large-scale defections. In 1989, the PCI had 1.4 million members; in its first year as the Democratic Party of the Left (Partito democratico della sinistra, or PDS), in 1991, it attracted under a million.[18] Meanwhile, in regional elections held in May 1990, the PCI received 24 percent of the vote, down from 30 percent in 1985. The steep drop was no doubt caused by a combination of factors, including the collapse of Communism in Eastern Europe, the unflattering publicity given to the bitter fights within the

PCI, and the party's inability to articulate a clear political program.[19] The electoral debacle, though, gave new ammunition to the "no" forces, who argued that the party's decline was due to Occhetto's leadership and, in particular, to the abandonment of the party's Communist identity and betrayal of its anti-capitalist principles.

The final showdown occurred under dramatic circumstances in late January 1991. The Twentieth Party Congress was convened just days after the United States led U.N.-sponsored military forces into Kuwait and Iraq. The PCI condemned this expedition, which played into the old imperialist imagery used by the party Left. Although Occhetto was again able to gather two-thirds of the delegates' votes for the end of the PCI and the foundation of the new Democratic Party of the Left, he was unable to prevent a minority from walking out and forming its own, still-proud-to-be-Communist party, the Rifondazione comunista. His victory was further sullied when, the day after the new party was formed, he initially failed to gather sufficient votes in the newly elected Central Committee to be chosen first head of the PDS. Although this was remedied a few days later, the party was off to an inauspicious start.

Now that the stage is set, it is time to begin our story. Although it tells of the transformation of the Italian Communist Party in the crisis years of 1989–91, readers looking for a standard account of the workings of the party, and the intricacies of the larger political system of institutions, elections, and power brokers, are likely to be disappointed. Many competent studies of this sort are already available, and doubtless others will soon be published. My concern is with the role of symbolism and the manipulation of history in the Communist struggle, and my central focus is the evolution of the party's Communist identity. I examine the anguish of the party members, whose personal identity was threatened, and the dilemmas faced by the PCI leaders who sought to unburden the party of its Communist associations. If this book shows the limits of this focus, the limits are happily chosen, for they stem from my belief that in modern national politics the role of symbolism is central.

chapter two

Making Communist History

The Italian Communist Party's appeal to members and sympathizers rested on various pillars. For many in the industrial working class, for example, the PCI's aggressive role in backing the union movement and fighting for workers' benefits over the years merited fierce loyalty. Yet we cannot understand the party's appeal without understanding its successful construction of history. This history was both outward looking—casting an eye on the rest of the world, producing a PCI view of world history—and inward looking, holding itself up for inspection, producing a self-history.

History is created in many different ways, but two processes especially stand out: mythologization and ritualization. Myths serve to give form to history, to provide it with a narrative structure and a coherence it would otherwise lack. Ritual, in contrast, provides not only a powerful mechanism for the propagation of myth—for socialization to myth—but also a framework in which myth itself can take shape. Rites not only reflect myth but also help produce it.

Myth and Ritual

As Lévi-Strauss noted many years ago, there is a deep and highly instructive paradox to be found in myth. Because myth depends on the manipulation of symbols, which can be of infinite variation—one can tell a myth about anything—we might suppose that myths found in different societies would be radically different. Yet what is most striking about myths are their uncanny similarities from society to society.[1]

In the political sphere, a handful of common themes underlie the most powerful myths worldwide. Grouped in what Gilbert

Durant refers to as *constellations mythologiques,* these themes are products of human insecurity and the need for faith. According to the French anthropologist Raoul Girardet, three of these themes are of particular importance in the construction of political myth throughout the world: (1) the existence of an evil conspiracy; (2) the existence of a Savior; and (3) the coming of a Golden Age.[2] It should hardly be surprising to find these themes in Italian myth, for they lie at the core of the Christian tradition, with its heaven and hell, good and evil, sin and salvation, and its millennial vision of the future.

Underlying Girardet's view is a psychological theory, with clear roots in the psychoanalytic tradition. We see this in his discussion of the human tendency to detect conspiracy. Stemming from "un obscur sentiment de menace, témoignage d'incertitude ou de panique" (a vague feeling of threat, testimony to a sense of uncertainty or panic), the mythology of the conspiracy, according to Girardet, is based on our tendency toward projection. People project onto the Other wishes and abilities that they cannot admit to or feel frustrated in achieving: the desire to have unlimited power, to act in perfect harmony and with perfect effectiveness with others of our kind against opponents, the ability, in short, to determine the course of history. Communist mythologization was driven by this Manichaean impulse: the division of the world and of history into, on one hand, evil conspirators operating on a vast scale and, on the other, a Savior whose good works promise to usher in the Golden Age.

It is revealing that Italy's most famous Communist thinker, Antonio Gramsci, recognized the role played by myth, identifying its political importance in an often-quoted passage from his work *The Prince* (a term he used in his prison notebooks as a euphemism for the Communist Party). "The basic thing about the Prince," wrote Gramsci, "is that it is . . . a 'live' work, in which political ideology and political science are fused in the dramatic form of a 'myth.'" He went on to argue, adopting Georges Sorel's view of myth, that the Prince could be seen as a "political ideology expressed neither in the form of a cold utopia nor as a learned theorising, but rather by a creation of concrete phantasy which acts on a dispersed and shattered people to arouse and organize its collective will."[3]

The PCI's founding myth focused on the Russian Revolution as the cataclysmic event destined to usher in the millennium. In this vision, the Soviet Union was seen as the embodiment of all that was good, struggling in a mighty battle against evil, namely, the forces of capitalism and imperialism epitomized by the United States.

Myth, though, can be socially constructed and propagated only through some kind of social mechanism. Those in power have a wide selection of means available for this purpose, from public schools to churches, radio programs, and television shows. For the first quarter century of its existence, the PCI had no such mass media. Indeed, even in subsequent years (that is, after the war), it had only limited access to these media. It is in this context that ritual loomed so large. Through party-sponsored ritual, the PCI mythological system and with it the PCI view of history spread and flourished.

The examples are numerous. Each year, for instance, the PCI published a party yearbook, which was distributed widely. The yearbook was one of the most evident signs of the importance that the PCI placed on its history: the book was an annual building block in the reification of history. The introduction to the *Almanacco PCI '77,* published at the historical high point of the party's electoral fortunes, provides a good example. Its emphasis is not on the party's unprecedented electoral victories of the past year. Rather, it concentrates on the party's key myths and symbols, the elements from which the party's history was to be constructed. The introduction to the volume directly links the proper understanding of current Italian political problems to proper "reflection on various historical processes (especially anniversaries: the thirtieth of the constitution, the fortieth of Gramsci's death, and the sixtieth of the October Revolution)." Historical processes are thus identified with the ritualizations of history: the ritual becomes the history.[4]

A key to this ritualization of history is the taming of time. The leaders of the French Revolution, themselves following ancient precedents from both Europe and Asia, had sought to put time to political use by identifying its passage with their own ideology. Mussolini followed this venerable tradition, insisting that the calendar be recalibrated to measure all time from the date of his accession to power. In this appropriation of time for instructional purposes, life is marked by temporal units that are given their meaning by selected political "events": PCI members were to view 1977 as the thirtieth anniversary of the postwar constitution, the fortieth of the death of Gramsci, and the sixtieth of the Russian Revolution. Each such symbolic marker furnishes a ritual rationale for development and communication of the myths that compose the party's version of history. The concluding section of the 1977 yearbook, labeled "History," consists of a series of photograph-rich articles with such titles as "The October Revolution," "Paths and Strategies of Socialism from 'October' to Today," and "1891–1937 Gramsci: Chronology of a Life."[5]

Although the PCI was in no position to alter the basis of the calendar (and, in any case, the memory of Mussolini's calendar was too fresh for the PCI to choose such a route), the party did do its best to create a calendar of its own for its members. This calendar was strewn with dates marking the party's construction of history. The most routine reports of party activities were framed in terms that underscored this party-dominated interpretation of time (and thus history).[6]

Take, for instance, a 1950 report to the national congress of the Communist Youth Federation (Federazione giovanile comunista italiana, or FGCI) on the recent membership drive. FGCI head (later to be PCI head) Enrico Berlinguer told the assembled multitudes, "In fact, while on July 14, 1949 (anniversary of the criminal attempt on the life of Comrade Togliatti), we had 214,677 members and 2,224 party sections, today thanks to the successive campaigns for the anniversary of the October Revolution, in honor of Comrade Stalin,

and in honor of the martyrdom of Eugenio Curiel . . . our federations have already brought in 375,212."[7]

No major PCI gathering could take place without this kind of
symbolic linkage to events in the past. Such a linkage not only fostered a certain view of the past but also legitimized the party and its
actions and leadership in the present. Typical in its apparent banal-
ity was the concluding resolution of the Eighth Congress of the PCI
Federation of the Province of Milan, held in 1954. The unanimously
approved resolution warned that the rearmament of West Germany
not only threatened Europe and Italy as a whole but also constituted
a "threat and a serious offense aimed at Milan, whose civic banner is
decorated with a gold medal for its heroic struggle against the Nazi
invader, and which today gathers, deeply moved and united in
remembering the tenth anniversary of the Resistance."[8] Here the
question of German rearmament is connected to the symbolic identification of Milan with a particular construction of history (as a
gold-medal winner, populated by heroic participants in the anti-
Nazi struggle), and that history is further made current by associat-
ing the congress itself with a marking of ritual time: the tenth
anniversary of the Resistance.

The public commemoration of anniversaries was a vehicle for
the party leadership to communicate both with the membership and
with the population at large. Through these commemorations the
party sought to establish its identity, to craft its view of history and
the party's relation to it, and to build popular allegiance to the PCI.

In places where the party was in power, such ritualization
enjoyed public sponsorship. To take a typical case, in 1973 an "extraordinary" session of the Provincial Council of Bologna was held to
celebrate the twenty-eighth anniversary of the Liberation of
Bologna. Speakers included representatives of the various "democratic" parties (that is, the "neo-Fascist" Italian Social Movement
[Movimento sociale italiano, or MSI] was excluded); the PCI's desig-
nated representative spoke "in the name of the Unitary Anti-Fascist
Committee of Provincial Employees." Immediately following the

ceremonies, which were held in the Provincial Council grand hall, a procession set out for the Shrine of the Partisans (Sacrario dei partigiani) in Bologna's central piazza. Nor was this all. Commemoration of the twenty-eighth anniversary led to a special provincial publication—containing the text of various speeches and an assortment of pictures both of the ceremonies and of events connected with the Liberation—and furnished the rationale for publishing a monthly series of special publications on the Resistance in Bologna, "dedicated to the celebrations connected to the thirtieth anniversary of the Resistance and the twenty-fifth anniversary of the constitution." Edited by the Bologna PCI's official historian, Luigi Arbizzani, these booklets were subsequently united in a single bound volume designed to be "distributed to libraries, schools, clubs, neighborhoods, hamlets, towns, etc."[9]

Another example of how the PCI used anniversaries—together with their close relation, annual holidays—to create history and nourish the party's symbolic universe is an event that took place in Tuscany in 1956. Roberto Giovannini, Communist mayor of the city of Prato, addressed a crowd assembled to celebrate the thirty-fifth anniversary of the founding of the PCI. It is worth looking at a goodly portion of his speech to see just how rich in myth, symbol, and the construction of history such ritual occasions were. As the applause that greeted him died down, he began:

Comrades, citizens!
... In your applause I don't see simply a formal act of courtesy directed at the person you see before you. ...
Comrades, I don't think I am mistaken: your applause, so warm, so sincere, so prolonged, represents an affectionate and enthusiastic tribute to our red flag, to that flag which is the symbol of our proletarian faith, to that flag which today is hoisted in front of the Communist sections in all the cities and the villages, fluttering in the wind in the skies of Italy to celebrate the thirty-five years of life, of struggles, and of victories of the Ital-

ian Communist Party, vanguard of the Italian people, and secure guide of the working classes of the Nation.

Your applause, comrades, is a tribute to Gramsci and to Togliatti, inspirational guides in the thought and action of all Italian Communists.

Your applause is a tribute to all the old comrades in Italy—both those who have been lost and those who have survived—who, thirty-five years ago at Livorno, gave birth to the party of the Italian working class in the struggle against Fascism, a struggle that was brought to a victorious conclusion.

Your applause is a fraternal tribute to all the old comrades of Prato who founded the Communist Party section of our City....

Your applause, comrades, is directed at Comrade Dino Saccenti. He is not here today. And we keenly feel his absence. As you know, he is currently in the Soviet Union, which is hosting him in order to lavish on him all the treatments necessary for his health, which has been undermined by the struggles that he waged against Fascism on all fronts, continuously, both in Italy and abroad. We send Comrade Saccenti the best wishes of all of us for his rapid return to his City, among his comrades, so that he can face new battles and achieve new and even more brilliant victories.

Your applause, finally, is a tribute to all the comrades in Italy, who are today celebrating . . . in order to mark the birth of our glorious party, January 21, 1921, the date which not only belongs to the history of a party but to the history of Italy, because from that moment a new force entered on the national political scene, a force which would have the greatest weight and prove to be the decisive element in the struggle against Fascist tyranny.

Giovannini then attempted to further connect the members present to the party's past:

Comrades!

Look at the symbol on our membership card this year. Remember, think back to the symbol of the cards of '21 and '22.

The party's first membership card had for its symbol a strong, self-confident worker, who held in his raised hands a hammer aimed at a world bound in chains.

And in '22 another symbol: a dangerous sea with heavy waves, and on this stormy sea an open book, rolling like a life raft. On this open book, on one side, "Communist Manifesto" is written and, on the other, the names "Marx-Engels." Rising above this life raft stood a worker who paddled an oar with one hand and held up a red flag with the other.

These first two membership cards, which the old comrades of '21 and '22 had, symbolized the struggles of their time: they were the symbols of the struggle against Fascism, they were the symbols of the struggle for the universal principles of human redemption enunciated by Marx and Engels.

Comrades!

Look, now, at the membership card that you have taken. There is a symbol on it: an open book, once again, an open book raised by the hand of a worker, and at the bottom two flags: the national tricolored flag and the red flag of our faith. On this open book . . . there is again something written: "Constitution—Workers' Rights—Peace."[10]

The instructional use of the party rites could hardly be more evident, the tone more didactic. Nor could there be much clearer examples of the use of ritual to formulate and communicate the central party myths. The mayor first evokes solidarity around the symbolism of the party by addressing his listeners as *compagni* and *compagne*. He indicates the proper objects for the crowd's enthusiasm, providing a litany of the holy symbols of the party. First comes the party's red flag, identified as the symbol of proletarian faith; the PCI itself is said to represent the sure guide of the working classes.

The patron saints of the PCI—Antonio Gramsci, party martyr, and Palmiro Togliatti, longtime party head—are identified and paid obeisance. The mayor then gives a rapid version of the origin of the PCI. Next, various local heroes are saluted, and even illness is used to mythic effect. The illness of Dino Saccenti, an elderly comrade of Prato, embodies the party myths both by requiring treatment in the USSR and by being diagnosed rhetorically as the product of a life devoted to anti-Fascist struggle. This tribute raises another important theme, namely, the predilection of the PCI for military metaphor. Saccenti's whole life, as a Communist, is portrayed as that of a soldier in the anti-Fascist cause: his health was undermined by anti-Fascist "combat," and he is urged back to health so that he can once again take part in new "battles" and achieve new "victories."

Finally, the mayor's anniversary commemoration is notable—though not unusual—for the self-consciousness with which it interprets the newest party symbol, the emblem found on the 1956 party membership card. By directly juxtaposing the new membership card with the original membership card of 1921, the continuity of the PCI is symbolically expressed, and the solidarity of current members with those founders is fostered. By focusing on the continuity of symbolism—the symbol of the powerful (male) worker, the iconic use of Marx's and Lenin's names, the hammer, the red flag, the *Communist Manifesto*—the holy power of the symbols is ritually recharged.

A large portion of party activities in the public arena consisted of the manipulation of symbols in ritual contexts, helping to identify the party in the public mind with certain images. Recall Berlinguer's speech to the national congress of the FGCI in 1950. At that time, and again two decades later during the Vietnam War, the PCI assigned the Communist Youth Federation the task of organizing anti-war activities and thereby identifying the party with the forces for world peace. This was accomplished through sponsorship of a vast network of ritual activities. Berlinguer could thus report in

1950 of the FGCI's great success over the past year, pointing with pride to four kinds of activities: (1) large demonstrations held in the spring against Italy's new membership in the North Atlantic Treaty Organization (NATO); (2) the inauguration of four thousand "peace flags," during which hundreds of thousands of youths "solemnly swore to defend the sacred cause of peace and national independence with all their might"; (3) the holding of fifteen regional and then one national conference for peace and liberty, involving huge public demonstrations; and (4) the response of the FGCI to the visit in Italy of the American "war ambassador" (a U.S. diplomat), who was greeted by massive street demonstrations, strikes, and protests by the youths in cities throughout much of the northern half of the country, and by the surreptitious hoisting of peace flags atop three American consulate buildings.[11]

The crucible in which the link between ritual and myth is forged involves the symbolic taming not only of time but of space as well. Endowing certain spaces with sacrality is universal in the struggle for power, as it is in governance. Space is marked off in a way that not only brings to mind a certain view of history but also links those in the present to that sacred past.

This sacralization of space by the PCI was most fully developed in the treatment afforded the Resistenza. In hamlets, towns, and cities throughout the northern half of Italy—which had been occupied by the Nazis in 1943—plaques were erected to mark the sites where partigiani had fallen. The fact that the Nazis and Italian Fascists had often used the central piazzas of cities for exemplary mass executions led the Communists and their allies to mark these spaces symbolically and use them for ritual commemorations. Indeed, there is some irony here, for the Nazis themselves, in their attempts to intimidate the local population, had chosen the central piazzas for their symbolic value.[12]

The sacrality of these spaces, which linked the PCI to Resistance mythology, was continually reinforced not only through the holding of commemorative ceremonies on the hallowed ground but also by preventing its ritual pollution. The PCI made highly publicized efforts to prevent the Fascists (that is, members of the MSI) from holding their own rallies in the sanctified central piazzas.

In 1960, for example, rioting broke out in Genoa when the MSI tried to hold its national congress in the center of the city, next to a memorial honoring partisans who had been executed by the Fascists a decade and a half before. The Genoa protest coincided with Communist demonstrations against the government, led by the Christian Democratic Party (Democrazia Cristiana, or DC), for its use of MSI votes in parliament to keep it afloat. Events in Genoa led to demonstrations throughout the country, with lethal results. The deaths that ensued in turn provoked a general strike, which forced the prime minister's resignation. What had started as a protest against the desecration of ritual space became a movement with major national political consequences, a movement that attracted a new generation of young people to the Communist Party.[13]

The Course of Italian Communist History

The PCI was born in 1921 as a result of decisions made by the Third International, itself strongly conditioned by the newly victorious Communist Party of the Soviet Union.[14] The Bolsheviks' victory had a tremendous impact on the socialist movement in Italy, as elsewhere in Europe, generating great enthusiasm for the world's first workers' state. The Third International specified that to become a member, a national party must—as the Soviet party itself had—expel all socialists who opposed a revolutionary Communist path to power. To demonstrate that they were but the local branch of an international organization, such parties were required to change their name to "Communist Party of . . ."

In the aftermath of the Russian Revolution, the Italian Socialist Party (Partito socialista italiano, or PSI), founded in 1892, was riven by conflict.[15] While most members continued to favor reformist objectives and were uncomfortable with the leadership of the Russian Communists and their call for a "dictatorship of the proletariat," many others found the Bolsheviks' example exhilarating. In May 1920, one such admirer, Antonio Gramsci, then leader of Turin's PSI section, attacked the PSI as a "petit bourgeois parliamentary party" and called for its transformation into a "party of the revolutionary proletariat which struggles for a future Communist society through a workers' state." He concluded, "Those who are not revolutionary Communists should be eliminated from the party."[16]

Matters came to a head in January 1921, amid a rising tide of Fascist violence and governmental instability, at the PSI national congress, held in Livorno. The Communist faction of the PSI, following its failure to win a majority, walked out of the congress and gathered in another Livorno hall. The story of this sacred procession was endlessly recounted a half century later, though the details varied. For example, the 1970 party yearbook had the secessionist delegates singing "Bandiera rossa" (Red Flag), while the yearbook of two years later had them singing the "Internationale."[17] These were to become the two most important songs of the party.

The new party, duly named the Partito comunista d'Italia, was voted into existence as a section of the Communist International. The name would be kept until 1943 when, in the wake of the dissolution of the Third International and in an effort to symbolize the Communists' patriotic allegiances, the name was changed to the Partito comunista italiano. As part of its founding act, the new PCd'I called for the destruction of the bourgeois state and the installation of a proletarian dictatorship, excluding the bourgeois class "from any political rights."[18] The Russian Revolution and its leaders became objects of adulation.[19]

A year after the founding of the PCd'I came the high point of the Fascists' own brand of political theater, the March on Rome. The march, which took place amid severe social tensions, labor unrest, Fascist violence, weak governmental leadership, and fears of Socialism, led to Mussolini's appointment as prime minister. Within a short time the Fascists dominated the government, and by 1926 the

PCd'I was driven underground. Gramsci was arrested that year, as were many other party members; the leaders who succeeded in escaping arrest fled the country. Some found refuge in France, but many went to Russia. Throughout these years of repression by the Fascist regime, Palmiro Togliatti remained head of the party, operating most of the time from Moscow, where he was also a key member of the secretariat of the Communist International.

By the late 1920s Togliatti was fully aware of the nature of Stalin's rule, and aware as well of the fate that awaited any who dared criticize him. In 1929, for example, one of the PCd'I delegates to the International, Angelo Tasca, was expelled from the party following his public disagreement with Stalin's policy. And in 1938, Togliatti's brother-in-law was interrogated and tortured by Stalin's police and spent a year and a half in a Russian jail, in an apparent effort by the Soviet authorities to gather incriminating information on the PCd'I leadership.[20]

In the PCI's later reconstruction, this was a heroic period for the party, in which it led the small but effective resistance to Fascist rule in Italy. In fact, however, the party was largely ineffectual in these years. Ironically, the most vocal complaints about its ineffectiveness came from the Moscow-based Communist International. At a meeting of the International's Political Secretariat in 1934, Osip Piatnitsky branded the PCd'I an "organization of the terrorist type without terrorism," adding that it "doesn't even know how to create a commotion." When, two years later, a PCd'I delegation returned from the Soviet Union to report to the Italian-based leadership on the sharp criticisms they received from the International Secretariat, the reaction was, in the words of Joan Urban, "one of sycophancy toward the Comintern authorities (Togliatti included), backstabbing among themselves, and an abject search for scapegoats. Each sought to shift responsibility for the party's purported deviations to others in the group."[21]

The same man, Palmiro Togliatti, would preside over the PCI both in its years as a small, illegal revolutionary party of cadres calling for proletarian dictatorship, and later, following the fall of Mus-solini, when the PCI became a mass-membership party embracing multiparty parliamentary democracy. This posed a symbolic prob-lem of considerable dimensions, one that could be resolved only via a transformation of history. Both Togliatti's previous role and the nature of the party itself had to be recrafted. The postwar battle between the PCI and its Italian opponents thus came to be fought in good part over history. It is hardly surprising that one of the vehicles that postwar opponents of the PCI used to attack the party was to identify Togliatti with Stalin and charge him with complicity in Stalin's crimes.

Togliatti was, in fact, one of the leaders of the Comintern dur-ing Stalin's Great Purges in 1937–38. Davide Lajolo, a veteran Com-munist Party leader and longtime friend of Togliatti, tells in his memoirs of confronting Togliatti shortly after reading a book that told an upsetting story. The book charged that, in the late 1930s, Togliatti was complicit in the execution of the leaders of the Polish Communist Party, whom Stalin had accused of being "Fascist spies and Trotskyists." In responding to Lajolo, Togliatti acknowledged the account's veracity but added, by way of self-defense, that had he not gone along with Stalin, he would have met the same fate as his Pol-ish colleagues.[22]

Back in Italy, after a brief flurry of activity in the early 1930s, the PCd'I's fortunes declined further, partly because of the debilitating effects of repeated arrests of activists, partly because of the vagaries of a political line dependent on Stalin's whims, and partly because of the popularity of the Fascist regime. Although in subsequent por-trayals the party would gloss over this fact, the PCd'I was at its nadir in the years preceding the collapse of the Fascist state (1939–42), its weakness compounded by the disorientation produced by the sign-ing of the German-Soviet nonaggression pact in August 1939.[23]

The luck of the PCd'I was soon to change, though, as the disas-trous consequences of Mussolini's decision to join the German war effort began to be felt. Although the PCd'I had had little success either in catalyzing popular opposition to the Fascist state or in building its own membership before 1943, it had a sufficient degree of organization to help fill the void left by the collapse of the Italian state in that year. Mussolini's fall had little to do with the PCd'I, coming primarily as a result of the regime's military reverses and, the final blow, the landing of Allied forces in Sicily in July 1943. It was only a matter of days after the arrival of Allied troops on Italian soil that Mussolini was overthrown by Fascist government leaders plotting with the king.

In the PCI's construction of history, however, the fall of Mussolini and, later, the defeat of the Nazi occupation were first and foremost the result of the efforts of the Communist Party. This history emphasized not the military actions of the Allied troops but the action of the PCI where it was strongest, among the industrial workers of Turin and Milan. Togliatti provided the classic PCI account of the events of 1943:

> On May 1, 1942, there was the first open agitation in Turin. In the following months the strikes began, whose number, in both Piedmont and Lombardy, increased every month. The organization of the party, meanwhile, extended to all Italy, and the clandestine press began to appear regularly. In March and April 1943, various large strikes broke out, beginning with Turin and Milan, in coordinated fashion, organized directly by the Communists. Hundreds of thousands of workers went on strike, and the movement threatened to extend to all parts of northern Italy. Fascism halted them with a series of economic concessions, but it was not able to prevent the profound effects that the movement had throughout the country. What the Communist Party had indicated as the essential objective began to be realized: the working class placed itself at the head of the Liberation struggle.[24]

In September, as the new Italian government negotiated terms with the Allies, the German army marched southward through the

Italian peninsula. The Germans freed Mussolini from his prison and took him north to Salò, where his puppet regime was installed. The new Italian government in Rome was overthrown, as the king ignominiously fled south to safety, and Nazi-dominated Fascist rule was imposed in its place. It would take the better part of two years for the Allies to clear the Nazis out of the rest of Italy, aided by Italian forces of what came to be known as the Resistance.

On the heels of the defeat of the Nazis and the puppet Mussolini government in 1945, many Communists—new and old—thought the time ripe for the proletarian revolution that the party had long espoused. The old government and bureaucracy had collapsed, the monarchy was severely compromised by its collaboration with Mussolini, housing in many areas was reduced to rubble, and the economy lay in ruins. Yet the party leadership, firmly under Togliatti's control, argued against a revolutionary path, warning that with large numbers of Allied troops still occupying the country it would be suicidal.[25]

Instead, the PCI publicly embraced multiparty, parliamentary democracy and, following the war, gave first priority to collaborating in the writing of a new, republican constitution. The membership grew at an exponential pace: from only a few thousand in all Italy in 1942, it skyrocketed to close to two million by the end of 1945.[26]

On July 14, 1948, however, the party's revolutionary proclivities were unleashed once again when a would-be assassin drove the Communist rank and file to the brink of revolt. At midday, a Fascist youth took four shots at Togliatti as he came out of parliament, leaving him close to death. As the news spread, violent demonstrations swept the country, and talk of insurrection grew. In Genoa, for example, an angry crowd took control of the armored cars of the riot police, while in Liguria ex-partigiani dug up the rifles they had hidden three years before. In Turin, workers took over the factories. In Milan, the police were disarmed when they attempted to assert control over workers at two of the city's major factories; elsewhere in the city irate throngs of workers laid siege to police headquarters. All over northern and central Italy, main roads were blockaded. When the national labor confederation, the Confederazione generale italiana del lavoro (CGIL), proclaimed an open-ended general national strike, many believed that the revolt of the proletariat was finally at hand.

In spite of the void left by Togliatti, the PCI leadership held fast to its line and did what it could to cool the ardor of those clamoring for armed revolt. As a result, after a few days of angry demonstrations, factory occupations, and heady talk of revolution, tensions diminished, and the leaderless forces of insurrection laid down their arms.[27]

The collaborative approach championed by the PCI in these years was on display in the drafting of the new Italian Constitution. The party surprised many observers, and angered many of its members, by voting for Article 7 of the constitution, reaffirming the 1929 pact between Mussolini and the Vatican, which established the Roman Catholic Church as the state religion and gave it state financial support. This vote was to become the showpiece of the PCI argument that, church claims to the contrary notwithstanding, the party was not anti-Catholic, and that Italians could be both Communist and Catholic.[28]

Communist participation in the national government was not to last long. As the Cold War intensified, a series of encounters took place in early 1947 between DC and American leaders. President Truman spoke of the dangers of Communism in Western Europe, and the American government promised the DC its support in efforts to exclude the Communists from national power. In this context, Prime Minister Alcide de Gasperi dissolved the coalition government and in May formed a coalition that excluded both the Communists and the Socialists.

The following year, in the first parliamentary elections of the new republic, the Christian Democratic Party soundly defeated a PCI-PSI coalition. The DC would continue its hold on the government for the next forty-five years, making use of a largely stable cast of smaller, allied parties, while the PCI was consigned to opposition.[29] By the early 1950s, when its electoral alliance with the Socialist Party came apart, the PCI had established itself as the second largest party in Italy, after the ruling Christian Democrats. It would retain this position until the tumultuous events of the early 1990s, when both the PCI and the DC would be radically transformed.

The early postwar years saw the construction of the PCI's impressive capillary organization. Party leaders recognized that the party's strength depended on its ability to mobilize and energize the membership and to spread the party's influence throughout Italian society. In this they drew on concepts of hegemony introduced by Gramsci, while preserving many of the organizational characteristics, such as democratic centralism, derived from their Leninist roots. "For every church tower a party section" became the slogan of the PCI, and the drive was largely a success. The party established thousands of sections throughout the country, each bustling with activity: on Sundays members went door-to-door selling the party daily newspaper, L'Unità; regular meetings of the membership discussed the political concerns of the day; and members gathered for periodic demonstrations in response to calls by the national leadership.

Every four years, the excitement of a national party congress energized all levels of the party, including the lowest, that of the section. The basis of each congress was a lengthy report (typically running a hundred pages or more) written by the national party secretary. The report was first discussed at party section meetings held throughout the country. These assemblies elected both local section officers and representatives to the next higher body, the federation congress (federations generally corresponded to the provinces). Present at each section congress was an emissary of the federation, who presented a summary of the national secretary's report and, in general, represented the hierarchy of the party to the local membership. Federation congresses were then held, electing representatives who ultimately composed the national party congress. The national congress was the major rite of the PCI, wherein the secretary's report would be enthusiastically accepted and members of the PCI Central Committee elected.

Although one of the main themes in the party's postwar presentation of its history was its absolute commitment to democratic principles, the Leninist-Stalinist roots of the party in the Third International were clearly on display in the actual congressional "debate." Under the banner of prohibiting factions and maintaining the unity of the party, sharp limits were placed on disagreement from the official party line, and the tradition of unanimous voting in every organ of the party was established, a policy that slowly began to erode only in the 1960s. Indeed, even throughout the 1970s, major changes in the policy of the party were made by the national leadership without any open discussion at all.[30]

The tone for the postwar years was set by an incident that took place in January 1951. At the provincial congress of the PCI Federation of Reggio Emilia, the head of the federation, Valdo Magnani, added to his report some comments critical of recent party policy. Reaction against him (and his colleague Aldo Cucchi, a PCI member of parliament from Bologna and a Resistance hero, who voiced his agreement with Magnani) was swift. After consultations with the national party leadership, the PCI Federation of Reggio Emilia expelled Magnani from the party. The language used by party leaders in this expulsion speaks volumes about the symbolic world in which the members of the party lived:

> Valdo Magnani, with the provocative action he engaged in at the party congress, where he intentionally tried to misrepresent the party's political line . . . sought in premeditated fashion to bring about the failure of the provincial congress. . . . Magnani . . . hid his actual intention, which was for criminal, factionalist ends. Magnani did not engage in this act out of any ideological conviction . . . but merely used this claim as a masquerade to

disguise his true treacherous action, trying in this way to hide the fact that he is an unprincipled renegade. . . . it has been established that Magnani, who spent many years living in Yugoslavia, has always maintained contacts with Titoist elements, provocateurs of betrayal . . . agents of imperialist and warmongering forces. . . . Magnani is a vulgar and despicable instrument in the hands of reactionary forces that have in such a way been able to infiltrate our party . . . in order to better strike the party at the time judged most opportune by his handlers.[31]

The party could not expel the dissenter for simply expressing his opinion, as this would contradict its democratic self-portrayal. To expel Magnani, the party had to transform him from one of "us" to one of "them," from friend to enemy, a conspirator against the party, the tool of foreign agents. Note, too, that in the context of the hottest internal party issue of the day, the vilification of the Yugoslavian leader (here again following Stalin's lead), the worst that could be said about Magnani was to link him to Tito. What had previously been regarded as one of Magnani's most important positive qualities—that he fought in the wartime Resistance in Yugoslavia—became a means for identifying him with the hated enemy.

This conspiratorial symbolism, wherein dissent equals betrayal, was quickly taken up throughout the party, as ranks closed around the leadership. Six weeks later, when the Federation of Milan held its congress, the PCI senator who gave the opening report noted, with satisfaction, that "our Federation reacted well to the treachery of Magnani and Cucchi, and gathered as one around the Direction of the party and Comrade Togliatti." The party must do whatever is necessary, the senator thundered, to stamp out the "criminal activity of enemy agents, spies, and provocateurs who may be hidden in our ranks."[32]

This type of discourse, and this model of organization, lasted for many years. Events of 1956—Khrushchev's secret report on Stalin, the incipient rebellion in Poland, and the Soviet invasion of Hungary—rather than undermine the symbolic world and mode of organization of the party, only fed the leadership's commitment to it, at least in the short run. Both the Polish and Hungarian cases were fitted into the existing conspiracy model. The revolts were portrayed as the work of a coalition of local reactionaries and foreign agents, bent on destroying the people's democracy and establishing a Fascist regime. What was most preoccupying about these events, in the eyes of the PCI leaders, was not what they revealed about life in Communist societies but, rather, how they were being used to discredit the Communist party.[33]

The Soviet invasion of Hungary was cast in the familiar mythological form of Soviet Union as Savior. Togliatti's description at the dramatic Eighth National Party Congress, held in late 1956, could hardly have been more firmly in this mold. He proclaimed that the outbreak of the revolt gave the imperialists hope that the "way was now clear to put their criminal designs into practice, now that the most powerful defender of peace, the Soviet Union, was paralyzed and public opinion disoriented." Togliatti continued, with satisfaction, to report that the imperialists' hopes had been dashed, thanks to the "severe warning aimed at the aggressors by the Soviet Union."[34]

As the worst of the Cold War tensions began to pass in the 1960s, the PCI position gradually changed. Party leaders sought to emphasize the PCI's independence from Moscow. This was not so much because of any concern over being identified with Soviet foreign policy. Rather, close association with the Communist countries undermined ongoing attempts to present the PCI as a Western party committed to multiparty government and civil liberties. In this context, Alexander Dubček's experimentation in Czechoslovakia with "socialism with a human face" received much praise, and when news of the Soviet invasion of 1968 reached Italy, the PCI was quick to denounce it.

Results of Elections in the House of Deputies, 1946–1987

Year	PCI (%)	PSI (%)	DC (%)
1946	18.9	20.7	35.2
1948*		31.0	48.5
1953	22.6	12.7	40.1
1958	22.7	14.2	42.4
1963	25.3	13.8	38.2
1968	26.9	14.5	39.0
1972	27.2	9.6	38.7
1976	34.4	9.6	38.7
1979	30.4	9.8	38.3
1983	29.9	11.4	32.9
1987	26.6	14.3	34.3

Source: Shore (1990:viii).
*In 1948 the PCI and PSI presented a joint slate of candidates for parliamentary elections.

This led to a new problem in the PCI's construction of its own history, as critics made much of the apparent contradiction between the party's criticism of the Soviet Czechoslovakian invasion and its approval twelve years earlier of the Hungarian invasion. Party leaders denied any such contradiction, arguing that the cases were entirely different: in Hungary there had been an "armed uprising" that "really placed the socialist government in danger," while in Czechoslovakia there had been no such threat.[35]

In spite of its somewhat equivocal nature, the new image of independence from the Soviet Union projected by the PCI proved successful in attracting broader electoral support. The accompanying table provides a summary of the vote in Italian general elections from 1946 to 1987, showing, in addition to the PCI vote, that of the Socialists and Christian Democrats.

Parliamentary election results from the early 1950s to the early 1970s show great stability, with the PCI taking about a quarter of the vote. This made it far and away Italy's second largest party, but left it well behind the Christian Democrats who, election after election, emerged the victors and excluded the Communists from governmental coalitions.

Party membership, however, did decline in the wake of the events of 1956. From 1954 to 1968, national membership sank by 650,000, from 2,145,000 to 1,496,000. The membership of the Communist Youth Federation (FGCI) dropped even more precipitously in this period, from 431,000 to 125,000.[36]

By contrast, the 1970s saw a boom in the PCI's fortunes, not only electorally but also in a surge in membership and greater visibility in society at large. Under the reformist leadership of Enrico Berlinguer, the PCI distanced itself further from the Soviet Union, a move symbolized most dramatically by Berlinguer's announcement that, after years of strident opposition, the PCI now welcomed Italy's continuing participation in NATO.[37] From the 1972 to the 1976 elections, the PCI increased its proportion of the vote by 25 percent, coming to within 4 percent of the DC.

In the regional and local elections of 1975, the Communists became the leading party in virtually all the nation's major cities. Before then, the PCI's electoral power—and control of local government—had been largely confined to the three central Italian regions of Emilia-Romagna, Tuscany, and Umbria. The 1975 elections extended the PCI majority not only to three other regions—Piedmont, Liguria, and Latium—but also to cities that, together, were the home of more than half the Italian population.[38]

These electoral successes energized the grass roots of the party. For the first time since the immediate postwar years, it was realistic to hope that the PCI could come to power nationally. Nothing better reflected the successful mobilization of the party membership in this period than the great upsurge in the party's most important local ritual occasions, the *feste dell'Unità*. These festivals, whose name derived from their role in raising funds for the party's daily newspaper (*L'Unità*), combined elements of traditional parish festivals with party symbolism (red flags, instead of images of patron saints, were held aloft). They equated the solidarity of the community with the symbolism of the PCI and placed the party member at the heart of the local community. Between 1972 and 1978, the number of such feste increased by 62 percent, with thousands being held throughout the country.[39]

Yet even at the height of the party's influence nationally, great regional differences in its organizational strength remained and, indeed, increased. For example, Emilia-Romagna and Tuscany, at the heart of Italy's "red belt," were together the home of 38 percent of PCI members in 1946. This proportion rose to more than 40 percent by 1980, although in that year the two regions were home to only 13 percent of Italians. In the same period, the proportion of PCI members living in the three northwestern regions of Piedmont, Lombardy, and Liguria—center of Italy's heavy industry and hence home of the classic proletariat—declined from 32 percent to 22 percent (in 1980 the three regions accounted for 27 percent of the Italian population). In 1980, in Italy as a whole, 4 percent of the adult population were PCI members, yet this figure varied from 2.5 percent in the south and 3 percent in Piedmont and Lombardy to 9 percent in Tuscany and 14 percent in Emilia-Romagna.[40]

Meanwhile, the PCI leadership, headed by party secretary Enrico Berlinguer, continued to distance the party from the Soviet Union. Matters culminated in a series of heated polemics following the imposition of martial law in Poland in 1981. In a famous pronouncement, Berlinguer argued that the Soviet model of socialism had exhausted its original progressive force and was not to be emulated. Indeed, he went so far as to equate the foreign policy of the USSR with that of the United States, charging both governments with following the logic of big-power-bloc politics rather than working for world peace. The Kremlin responded with bitter denunciations of the PCI leadership, although a formal break in relations was avoided. A number of observers identify this period as a time when the Soviet Union began funding the publications of the pro-Soviet minority within the PCI, which was headed by Armando Cossutta. When Cossutta's forces, however, introduced motions opposing the PCI leadership's critical stance vis-à-vis the USSR, they never succeeded in garnering more than about 15 percent of the votes of the membership.[41]

In spite of the party's efforts to show its full independence from the Soviet Union, its electoral support continued a decline that had begun with the 1979 parliamentary elections. Yet even at the end of the 1980s, when Party Secretary Achille Occhetto announced his proposal to transform the party, the PCI was still the second largest party in Italy and occupied more than a quarter of the seats in parliament; it remained the only serious competitor to the Christian Democrats.

chapter three

Saviors and Conspirators

Leaders of the Italian Communist Party, in developing the party's symbolic world, worked tirelessly to construct its history. Through these efforts, party leaders sought to define the party's identity (and hence the identity of its members), legitimize their actions and their leadership, and create a world in which current events could be properly interpreted.

Good Versus Evil

At the heart of the PCI's symbolic world was the Manichaean tradition of the international Communist movement. Present from the movement's nineteenth-century origins, it sprang from much earlier Christian roots. On one side lay good, on the other evil. On one side, the Communists; on the other, the capitalists and imperialists, Fascists and traitors. On the side of all that is virtuous, the Soviet Union; on the side of all evil, the United States.

Bringing together the most diverse list of enemies into a seamless web of evil conspirators was a hallmark of PCI rhetoric in the postwar period, a kind of symbolism mirrored in the 1950s in the anti-Communist crusade in the United States, Italy, and elsewhere in the West.[1] Togliatti's opening address to the 1951 national congress of the PCI was typical. He spoke of an "abyss" between socialism, which "opens the possibility of peace throughout the whole world," and imperialism, which "condemns the entire world of those countries dominated by American imperialism to anti-Communism, which was the mark of Nazism and of the Fascists on the eve of the Second World War."[2]

Enrico Berlinguer likewise propagated this worldview in the
early postwar years. In his introduction to the national FGCI congress
in 1950, for example, he painted an apocalyptic picture of the United
States and its allies:

> The American millionaires, ever more eager for profits, driven
> by the insane and crazy goal of becoming the world's masters,
> and in the illusory hope that preparation for war and war
> itself—even though it would result in unimaginable grief and
> ruin—would give them mastery of the universe, are preparing
> new aggression.
>
> The crazy, vile servants of the imperialists who write in the
> European press on their orders indeed speak today of "inter-
> planetary wars," of the movement of "solar masses." Their goal
> is to frighten and blackmail people who have weak nerves, to
> justify the arms race, and to distract people's attention from the
> struggle to ban atomic energy.
>
> The worst reactionary forces in the world, from the Span-
> ish to the Italian and German Fascists, from the clerical obscu-
> rantists of the Vatican to the right-wing traitors of social
> democracy and Tito-Tanković's band of spies and assassins,
> quaking in fear before the advance of the people, are today coa-
> lesced around the Anglo-American imperialists.
>
> These are the criminal plans of the provocateurs of war who
> month after month cast their awful threat of destruction over
> all humanity.

Having thus portrayed the evil conspirators, their hands dripping
with blood, Berlinguer cheered his audience by reminding them that
they had a Savior, ready to come to the rescue:

> In reality the system of threats and blackmail does not intimidate
> the Soviet Union and the democratic countries, who firmly pur-
> sue their policy of defending peace. The USSR needs peace in order
> to realize its economic plans and to save humanity. Its foreign pol-

icy is based on the principle of peaceful coexistence and competition between the socialist and capitalist systems. Yet, at the same time, the leaders of the Soviet state have warned the imperialists that if they dare unleash a new war, they would provoke such a massive popular reaction that it would wipe imperialism and aggression once and for all time from the face of the earth.[3]

Here Berlinguer mercilessly vilifies American capitalists, European social democrats, Tito, the Catholic Church, and others, casting them as partners in a worldwide conspiracy of evil. In contrast stands the Soviet Union, defender of peace, champion of all that is good. The image of the Great Conspiracy versus the Savior could hardly be more vivid.

The viciousness of the PCI's language and the Manichaean quality of its symbolism in these Cold War years reached their apogee when a former ally was to be repudiated. In such cases, the ally had to be shifted from the world of good to that of evil. Stalin's excommunication of Tito produced many examples of this treatment of those guilty of breaching the sacred solidarity of the Communist movement. The 1951 expulsion of Valdo Magnani provides one such instance. And three years later, in his introduction to the Seventh National Party Congress, Togliatti continued to denounce the "passage of Tito's gang to the imperialists' camp."[4]

In 1956, Party leaders employed this image of an embattled force for good surrounded by the forces of evil to rally the membership in the face of withering attacks on the party. The national party commission in charge of the annual membership drive issued a directive to all party sections in November of that year, warning that the "reactionary and Fascist pack of dogs has been unleashed against the party of the Italian Communists, in support of the imperialist forces of aggression and war." The directive went on to say that, under such circumstances, it was a "duty of honor" of all party members to renew their membership.[5] For the most part, indeed, the members heeded the call.

A supplementary symbolic strategy involved the collapsing of historical time, in an effort to equate criticisms of the PCI for its support of the Hungarian invasion with the gunshots aimed at Togliatti eight years before. The opening report to the Milanese Federation Congress of November 30, 1956, juxtaposed the two situations: "In July 1948, at the very moment when American imperialism was making our country into a military base for the Atlantic bloc, a vile attempt was made on the life of Comrade Togliatti. And even today the attacks of the Fascists, the clerics, and the reactionaries of every stripe are directed against our party and its leadership."[6]

The Military Metaphor

As reflected in the privileged position given to the war of good against evil in postwar Communist discourse, the symbolic world of Italian Communism relied heavily on a military metaphor (as did the *Communist Manifesto*). History was portrayed as an ongoing battle. Luigi Longo, vice secretary of the PCI, in his opening speech to the Seventh National Congress in 1951, proclaimed, "The history of these past three decades . . . is the history of this struggle . . . of the workers, the agricultural day laborers . . . to rebuff and defeat the offensive of the bosses and the imperialists." He hailed the sacrifice of the workers and the peasants whose blood had been "abundantly shed at the hands of the police, the rural landowners, and actual Fascist bands." Mixing in a dash of nationalism, Longo, in a rousing conclusion, called on the "popolo" to take action to achieve "victory against their enemies and against the enemies of peace, progress, and the greatness of the nation."[7]

The same military symbolism runs through Berlinguer's address to the PCI national congress that year. As head of the FGCI, he spoke with pride of the party's strides in obtaining the "greatest successes in the struggle . . . being fought between the reactionary forces and the democratic forces of the country to conquer the younger generations."[8] The previous year, in addressing the FGCI national congress, he had portrayed the Communist Youth Federation as blessed by a "glorious past," marked by "passionate battles" that the young proletariat "have been fighting for more than forty years."[9]

The Resistance looms large in the development of this military metaphor. PCI leaders regularly sought to equate the party's current political campaigns with the armed struggle of the Resistance. During the 1951 national congress, for example, the party head for the central region of the Marches urged the formation of a "vast national front, similar to the one that we succeeded in creating under Fascism and during the war of national liberation, a front that yesterday enabled us to liberate our country from the Fascists and the German troops and that today will allow us to liberate it from its submission to American imperialism."[10] Here, too, reference is made to the alliances formed during the Resistance: the Communist-Socialist alliance pushed by the PCI in 1951 was sanctified by the alliance of anti-Fascist forces that fought the Nazis. In this worldview, political opponents in Italy were simply branded "reactionary forces in the service of foreigners," in a discourse equating current domestic political adversaries with the foreign military adversaries of the war.[11]

Hagiolatry

The PCI's symbolic world was also marked by a strong tendency to sacralize its leaders, creating a pantheon of Communist saints. Not only were their names continuously invoked, but photographs of their faces had iconic value. Such photographs graced all party section headquarters and many public party activities.[12] These saints had the power to bestow their blessings on whatever political line was being espoused at the time, and to help legitimate those who invoked them. In a typical phrase of this sort, Togliatti, in 1955, instructed his audience, "Lenin, Stalin, Mao Tse-tung, the leaders of the socialist, popular movement in both West and East, are united in a common way of thinking, which is that begun by Karl Marx and Frederick Engels."[13] Togliatti's own apotheosis came upon his death in 1964, when more than a million people crowded into the streets of Rome for his funeral.[14]

Of course nothing is original in this practice, nor does it separate the Italian Communists from many other political groups around the world today or in the past. This hagiolatry, which reached its height in the 1950s and later began to diminish, gave PCI discourse a religious flavor, with historical references mixed with professions of faith. Take, for example, the segment of Berlinguer's 1950 FGCI speech in which, in a single convoluted sentence, he both identified the PCI as the "Leninist party of Gramsci and Togliatti" and attributed the FGCI's success to its record of "always remaining faithful to the country of victorious revolutionary socialism [that is, the USSR], to the immortal and invincible cause of Lenin and Stalin." His ninety-four-page speech ended, appropriately, with the chants (presumably each met by a thunderous "viva" from his audience) of "Viva our powerful and glorious FGCI! Viva Togliatti! Viva Stalin!"[15]

Two decades later, as vice secretary of the PCI, Berlinguer would, of course, no longer invoke Stalin's holy aura, but he continued to quote reverentially from Lenin and paid regular obeisance to "our great teacher, Antonio Gramsci."[16] Indeed, Berlinguer's use of the saints of the Communist past was something of a masterpiece of sacred descent. At the Twelfth National PCI Congress in 1969, for example, he introduced a quote from Togliatti by saying that the passage represented "one of the highest points achieved in the elaboration of Marxism in Italy, that Marxist vision that came from Labriola [the late-nineteenth-century socialist philosopher] and that, via Lenin, passed on to Gramsci and to Togliatti."[17]

Togliatti's own prestige and legitimacy were strongly reinforced by his studied efforts to be seen as the bearer of the sacred flame passed down by Gramsci. Togliatti regularly served as official party interpreter of Gramsci. Indeed, he was more than this: he became the guardian of Gramsci's shrine, the oracle through whose lips Gramsci could still speak.

This role did not end with Togliatti's death. Shortly after he died, the party press published a collection of Togliatti's writings on Gramsci. In his introduction to the volume, Ernesto Ragionieri took a defensive tack. Rather than deny the undeniable—that Togliatti had invented a history of Gramsci to suit his own political purposes—Ragionieri sought to treat this as unremarkable: "Today's reader should not and cannot be surprised that, at times, elements of legend, closely connected to the battles that were waged and to the myths that formed in the course of these battles, crept into this tradition." Questioning the right of any of today's readers to criticize this political use of history, Ragionieri proclaimed, "Only the Pharisean priests . . . who always claim to be on the side of truth in the case of others while, in their own homes, they keep and worship without a second thought the most faded icons and the most aged idols, dare show indignation over the fact that the political tradition of a revolutionary party is one and the same thing with the banner in whose shadow it has fought."[18]

Ragionieri went on to admit, for example, that in Togliatti's famous eulogy for Gramsci, given in 1937, he had presented some elements of Gramsci's biography "not without some simplifications." Among these simplifications, presumably, was Togliatti's presentation of Gramsci as a "son of poor peasants."[19] Togliatti at the time certainly knew that this was not true; in fact, Gramsci's father had been a law student at the university and had a job in the state bureaucracy; his mother was the daughter of a tax collector.[20]

Gramsci's death, following years of imprisonment by the Fascist regime, was likewise used to elevate him to sacred status. In Togliatti's account, Gramsci, given the opportunity to be released from jail if he would only plead personally to Mussolini for clemency, refused, thus ensuring his death.[21] Togliatti's historical accounts of Gramsci can be best read in the light of the political conflicts prevailing at the time Togliatti was writing. For example, in his 1937 article eulogizing Gramsci, Togliatti attributed Gramsci's election in 1915 as head of the Turinese section of the PSI to the "recognition of the part he had played in preparing the Turinese workers to understand the Russian Revolution, to understand and to love its leaders, Lenin and Stalin." Gramsci was thus assigned precocious awareness—this was, after all, two years before the Russian Revolution—that Stalin would share equal credit with Lenin for the Bolsheviks' success.[22]

The weaker the empirical basis for the claim being made by a PCI speaker, the more likely the speaker was to seek legitimation by invoking the party's sacred genealogy. In this, the Communists were acting no differently than politicians throughout the world, legitimizing their actions by references to a hallowed past. To cite one example, in 1969, Luigi Longo, then secretary of the PCI, wrote in the following terms about the party's firm democratic tradition: "A unity that is imposed from above, in the name of a doctrine that has become a dogma, is totally extraneous to us, to the conception, the history, and the practice of our party, the party of Gramsci and of Togliatti."[23]

Such references also occurred with notable frequency at transition points, when a change in party policy was being announced to the membership. The change of line had to be sanctioned by the party deities. A good example comes from 1971, when Alessandro Natta, who would later serve a short spell as national party secretary, was asked to write an account for party members of the decision at the end of the war to turn the PCI into a mass-membership party. He faced the awkward task of discussing how the party abandoned its revolutionary path and embraced what it had previously vilified as bourgeois democracy (that is, multiparty parliamentary government). He argued that Lenin would be the first to laugh at the notion that the path taken by the Russian people in 1917 should be "mechanically" applied under other circumstances, and then went on to cite Togliatti's statement to similar effect, before concluding by mentioning a 1926 article by Gramsci which, according to Natta, made the same point.[24]

The Myth of the Resistance

In the universe of PCI symbolism, the Resistance stood above all else as the source of legitimation of both the party's past and its present. Through the myth of the Resistance the PCI effected its transformation from a small, cadre, internationalist party essentially taking orders from Moscow to a large, mass-membership national party. The Resistance, properly presented, allowed the PCI to cast itself as the Savior of the nation.

If the party was the Savior, so too were those leaders who could lay claim to having fought in the Resistance. Part of their political work in later years consisted in doing what they could to keep the memory of the Resistance alive. Aside from promulgating the idea that there had been a coordinated military effort that could properly be described in unitary terms as "la Resistenza," the PCI architects of the Resistance myth emphasized three themes: (1) that the Resistance forces consisted principally of Communists;[25] (2) that, however, the Communists worked collaboratively and amicably with non-Communists;[26] and (3) that the defeat of the Nazis and their Fascist allies was, first and foremost, the result of the efforts of these Resistance forces.[27]

Although PCI accounts could not ignore the fact that in 1943–45 the nation was being progressively occupied by Allied military forces, the identity of those troops was often concealed and their role minimized. A PCI booklet devoted to the "great choices in the history of the PCI" is typical: "In July 1943, the Fascist regime crumbled under the weight of military defeat and the action of the popular and democratic workers' movement, which was continually gaining momentum." The booklet, reflecting the party's conundrum in dealing with the inconvenient presence of American and British troops at this mythic time, went on to explain:

> The war of Liberation took place in a contradictory context, in the sense that alongside the decisive intervention of the working class in the struggle came the appearance of the imperialist

forces in the country, the Anglo-Americans. Although they were unsuccessful in preventing the Liberation struggle from assuming the character of a national war, they nonetheless did succeed, once Liberation had taken place, in placing the Italian capitalist bourgeoisie under the protection of the occupation armies, helping them to recuperate their forces, limiting the conquest of democratic liberties, and reining in the drive of the workers toward essential political and economic reforms.

The booklet's account concluded by admitting that the "Allies' aid was essential for the liberation and independence of the country," yet added, "but this same independence, together with the new democratic liberties, was immediately threatened by their very presence."[28]

Rather than portray the Allied forces as heroes, the PCI sought to paint them, especially in the late 1940s and early 1950s, as, down deep, enemies of the Italian people. Two years after Liberation, for example, Togliatti told those assembled for the congress of the PCI Federation of Milan that although Italy had come out of the war "ruined and torn up," it was "less ruined and less torn up than the American and English imperialists had expected." The credit for this was clear: "Thanks to our Liberation forces, we succeeded in saving most of our industrial base," he said, adding darkly, "and this was a great surprise for everyone, which pleased us very much, but I don't know if everyone was equally pleased."[29]

To promulgate the myth of the Resistance, the party sponsored an annual series of commemorations of Resistance battles, martyrs, and victories. The cities where Resistance battles were fought were each presented with a Medaglia d'oro (a gold medal) and thereafter referred to in PCI rhetoric as "gold-medal cities."

A typical commemoration shows how the Resistance symbolism was promulgated. The occasion was the celebration of the thirtieth anniversary of the beginning of the Resistance, sponsored by the Committee for the Thirtieth Anniversary of the Resistance and

Liberation. In addition to organizing the official rites, the sponsors packaged the rites in a booklet, which was distributed throughout the province. Its opening passage quotes from the citation prepared for an earlier ritual occasion, when Bologna was awarded its gold medal: "Partisan city faithful to its ancient traditions, refusing to allow itself to be subjected to the arrogance of the German invader. And with the purest blood of thousands of its sons, with its houses destroyed, and through epic, protracted battles fought with arms taken from the enemy, it was at the vanguard of the uneven struggle and the insurrection which, in the radiant dawn of April 1945, reconquered the Nation's freedom. September 1943–April 1945." Such flights of rhetoric were common in ritualized presentations of the Resistance.

The Soviet Savior

By the late 1960s, a major theme of the PCI's presentation of its history was that the party had always been entirely independent from the Soviet Union. The question of Stalin and the PCI's relations with the USSR during the party's first three decades was, where possible, simply ignored. When the issue could not be avoided, the authors of PCI history portrayed the party as having always had a healthy, critical attitude toward Stalin and having always been critical of the "undemocratic elements" of Soviet rule.

A sensitive element of this history was the signing of the nonaggression pact between Hitler and Stalin in 1939. Party leaders tried to turn the uncomfortable episode to good effect as a lesson that the ways of the Soviet Communist leadership, although they might first seem contradictory, always proved right in the end. In this vein, Togliatti, trying to cope with the disquiet in the party's ranks in 1956 in the wake of Khrushchev's revelations about Stalin's brutality, recalled the similar disquiet produced by Stalin's signing of the pact with Hitler and concluded, "History rapidly showed we had been entirely right."[30] Here Togliatti referred to the PCI's claim that the pact was a necessary expedient, giving the USSR time to organize its forces to take on the Nazis.

Stalin's image as Savior was nourished in the immediate postwar years by the constant incantation of his heroic role in defeating the Nazis. Joan Urban, in her study of PCI relations with the USSR, linked the deification of Stalin and the idolization of the Soviet Union to the polarizing pressures of the Cold War. These pressures, she argued, "led the Italian Communist leaders actively to cultivate anti-Americanism and its mirror image, pro-Sovietism."[31]

Even before the onset of the Cold War, in the immediate aftermath of World War II, the party had seized on the USSR's wartime role to build the myth of the Soviet Union as defender of the world's workers and chief champion of world peace. In the fall of 1945, for example, with Soviet troops occupying much of Eastern Europe, party leader Mauro Scoccimarro proclaimed that Russia was the "only country in the world that will never be imperialist" and went on to say that the USSR was the "only country in the world in which politics means liberty, progress, civilization."[32]

In portraying the Soviet Union as the hero of the war, PCI leaders had to acknowledge that the only foreign troops that most Italians had ever seen fighting the Nazis were the Americans and British. Somehow, the presence of the armies of the bourgeois powers had to be integrated into the PCI's historical account. Togliatti, in a speech given in 1947, showed how this was to be done. The opponents of Nazism and Fascism in the war were, he said, a "heterogeneous front." On one side was the Soviet Union, a "socialist country, the nation having the most advanced democracy, which could not and cannot have any goals other than crushing the international reactionary Fascist forces, resisting and battling imperialism, defending the independence of all peoples, and protecting peace." Alongside the USSR, Togliatti went on to say, were very different forces, "of capitalist and imperialist countries," who were fighting not because of any principle but simply because they thought that the "banditry and . . . the crimes of Hitlerism and Fascism" had gotten out of hand.[33]

The postwar PCI panegyrics to the USSR and to Stalin would later prove embarrassing to the party and were absent from the multitudinous historical pamphlets on this period published in the late 1960s and the 1970s. The concluding paragraph of the final report voted by the 1951 national PCI congress was typical of the party language of the time: "The Seventh PCI Congress expresses its unshakable faith in the Soviet Union, bulwark of peace, guide and example for the peoples in all the world, and in its great leader, Comrade Stalin!"[34]

Stalin's death in 1953 (referred to in party publications of the time, in capital letters, as the "Grande Scomparso"—the Great Death, or the Great Departed) provoked a tremendous outburst of ritual activity and the frenzied construction of party myth.[35] To Stalin were attributed divine qualities, as we can see in Luigi Longo's parting tribute:

Stalin is dead . . . his titanic work, his genius, his life have for more than three decades astonished the world and won for his person the gratitude and the infinite care of the peoples. A third of humanity, eight hundred million people, thanks above all to his guidance and his example, have once and for all eliminated the exploitation of man by man; they have been liberated from all servitude and have taken their destiny firmly into their own hands . . .

The name of Stalin has been for so many years, for all of us, the beloved name of master, of teacher, and of leader, for so many years an incentive and comfort in the fight, an assurance of victory. . . .

We have the good fortune of having a great leader: Comrade Togliatti, the great pupil and friend of Stalin. Under his guidance we will know how to be victorious in the tasks that await us, we will know how to fulfill all the commandments left us by Stalin.[36]

In the PCI view, the Soviet Union was a paradise on earth; indeed, the millennial imagery is striking. In his speech to the national FGCI congress in 1950, for instance, Berlinguer proclaimed, "We struggle so that in Italy too a social and political system arises in which, as in the Soviet Union, youths are able to sing, to joke, and to make one another smile, and so that we can take charge of time, space and the future and become the masters of the universe [*padroni dell'universo*]."[37]

The early postwar period also saw the founding of the PCI–allied Italy–USSR Association, which would continue its work into the 1980s. Its goal was "encouraging a vast movement of sympathy and friendship for the Soviet Union among all segments of the Italian population."[38] This group, and parallel organizations for other Eastern European countries, organized tours for Italians to enjoy low-cost vacations in the Soviet Union, East Germany, and other Communist states.

The portrait of complete social harmony existing within and among the Communist-ruled nations offers a lesson in utopian geography. Take Togliatti's 1955 portrait of the world of socialist countries. He began by identifying this world as consisting of the USSR—characterized as a "federation of sixteen autonomous republics"—together with six European countries, the People's Republic of China, and three other Asian nations. It is a vast territory, Togliatti said, containing hundreds of millions of people. He went on: "These States and these people live in peace, they have no conflicts among them." Rather, the PCI leader explained, "they are engaged in a peaceful process of development and seek, with everyone's participation and energies, to . . . increase the well-being of all." He concluded by pointing out that these are the countries that most quickly overcame the tremendous damage caused by the Second World War "and that today are undeniably in the vanguard."[39]

Although events of the following year—not to mention the impact, somewhat later, of the China-Soviet rift—would make such portraits of Communist harmony increasingly untenable, the glorification of the USSR continued well into the 1960s. These panegyrics typically made implicit, if not explicit, comparisons of the USSR with the United States, showing the first to be superior in every respect. The opening sections of the 123 pages of theses prepared as a platform for the Ninth PCI National Congress in 1960, for example, report that the USSR had bested the most advanced capitalist countries in education, technology, science, and space exploration. In a short time, the platform continued, the USSR would overtake the United States in per capita wealth.[40] Such predictions were an oft-repeated point of pride for the PCI.[41]

In the 1960s, in the face of continuing evidence of the economic weaknesses of the Soviet Union, PCI leaders shifted the focus of discussion away from the economy. They increasingly turned instead to science as the proving ground for the superiority of Soviet society. Again, the matter was phrased competitively, pitting the USSR against the United States in a battle for not only political but moral supremacy.

In his introductory speech to the PCI national congress in 1969, Longo, as national party secretary, spoke on this topic. It is said, Longo began, that the United States—"where more than in any other country the law of private profit and of the great monopolies prevails"—is today the world's leader in science and technology. But, he argued, the USSR, starting from a much weaker position, had achieved much more. His equation of scientific superiority with political superiority is clear: "It is a fact that a quarter of all the world's scientists today work in the Soviet Union, in five thousand research institutes. This shows the level at which the battle between the two social systems is being waged, that between the socialist and the capitalist." Good, he said, would triumph over evil, and the PCI would forever stand with the virtuous: "We are on the side of the October Revolution, of the USSR and all the socialist countries, whose function has been and continues to be fundamental to the salvation of peace, liberty, and the world's future."[42]

By the late 1970s, when Sputnik's luster had worn off and the American predominance in space and in other scientific fields became more difficult to deny, the PCI looked to yet other grounds for comparison. The United States was portrayed as a society riven by crime, drugs, racial prejudice, and environmental pollution. Continuing a refrain heard from the time of the party's foundation, PCI leaders described capitalism as in a state of crisis, its contradictions threatening to produce imminent economic and social collapse.[43]

The PCI's domestic opponents peppered the party with the charge that although the Communists claimed to be for peace, they never criticized positions or actions of the Soviet Union in international affairs. In a typical response, Luigi Longo declared in 1962 that this was simply not true. The PCI, he said, denounces actions favoring war from whatever source they come. Although he admitted that "we have almost always found ourselves against the acts and facts of American imperialism and in favor of the acts and facts of the Soviet Union and the socialist countries," he argued that this was not surprising. The reason was simply "because it is in the nature of imperialism in general and of American imperialism in particular to be the promulgator of bellicose initiatives and war, of violence against other peoples." By contrast, "it is in the nature of the socialist countries to promote only peaceful initiatives and peace, and solidarity with other peoples."[44]

The Great Conspirator

In the immediate postwar period, PCI attempts to portray the United States as the Great Conspirator, source of all evil, suffering, and war, faced a variety of obstacles. These included both the recency of the American role in ridding Italy of the Nazi occupiers—and thus the clear link of the United States to the already mythical Resistance—and the American role in providing economic aid to the war-devastated nation.

These two problems were dealt with in quite similar ways. Party leaders adopted a dual historico-genic (history-producing) strategy in making sense of the American role in liberating Italy. The preferred alternative was simply to ignore it (a form of historical erasure), thus giving the impression that it was the PCI-sponsored Resistance that brought about the Nazis' defeat in Italy, while the Soviet Union was responsible for the Nazis' collapse elsewhere. When it was impossible to ignore the Allied role, PCI leaders, while acknowledging significant Allied involvement in the Nazi defeat, cast aspersions on the Americans' motives. Accordingly, Togliatti dismissed the Americans as "reactionary imperialists who intervened in the war solely with the intention of creating a situation in which it would be possible for them to realize their dream of world domination."[45]

The party confronted the problem posed by American economic aid to Italy in a similar fashion. First, party leaders denied that any significant amount of aid had been given. Second, they portrayed the aid that had been given as a crass attempt by the Americans to buy the allegiance of the Italian people for their anti-Communist crusade.

The first approach was on display in 1947. Togliatti informed party members that Winston Churchill and the American leaders had met after the war and decided to do as little as possible for Italy's economic reconstruction, limiting their aid solely to the "minimum essential so that we would not all die of hunger."[46] A few years later, Togliatti reported that U.S. economic aid had been designed only to turn Italy into an "American economic and political satellite" and would afford "in no case any improvement in the country's situation." He predicted that Italy's economic situation would become increasingly desperate.[47] "American imperialism," proclaimed Berlinguer in the same period, was in the process of transforming Italy into a "colonial country, without any industry of its own."[48] The same theme echoed throughout the party hierarchy: American imperialism had intervened to enable the discredited Italian "reactionary classes" to reestablish their control of the country. In exchange, in the words of Mauro Scoccimarro, member of the national secretariat, the "privileged groups sacrifice national independence, placing Italy at the service of the plans of aggression and war of foreign imperialism."[49]

Along similar lines, the party's dramatic defeat by the Christian Democrats in the first parliamentary elections held under the new constitution in 1948 was blamed on the United States. Togliatti branded the elections a fraud, claiming that foreign intervention had taken place on a scale never before witnessed anywhere. The Americans, Togliatti claimed, not only threatened the people with hunger if they voted for the Communists but threatened them with war as well. Indeed, according to him the Americans were "even—incredible though it may seem—threatening to use the atomic bomb against certain cities and regions, if the votes of the Communist-Socialist alliance prevail in those areas." Although the level of hyperbole was high, and the last claim reminiscent of the clerical stories of Communists eating babies, Togliatti had good reason to complain, for U.S. secret services had actively worked in concert with the Christian Democrats to defeat the Communist-Socialist alliance.[50]

By the 1970s, the impact of mass media, from popular music to movies and, especially, television, made the United States seem extremely attractive to many Italians, especially the young. The implied comparison with the Soviet Union did not work in the PCI's favor.

The PCI dealt with this threat to its youth recruitment by seizing on young Americans identified as martyrs to the evils of American society, allowing young Italians to celebrate American culture while attacking the American government and economy. The Vietnam War was particularly valuable: on one hand, party leaders used it to show the imperialist and warmongering nature of American society; on the other, the American anti-war movement provided a proper object for party approval.

Angela Davis, young, female, black, and, most significantly, a member of the Communist Party of the United States, was an icon for the Italian Communists. When she was jailed in the United States, PCI-sponsored demonstrations were held throughout Italy. Her picture seemed to be everywhere, as she was practically adopted by the Communist Youth Federation. The head of the FGCI, at the organization's national congress in 1971, commented, "And I would like to direct a greeting to Comrade Angela Davis, the pride of all the Communist youths worldwide, shining symbol of the other, democratic and anti-imperialist America." He then went on to address Richard Nixon as "president of the country that assassinated, to its eternal and ineradicable shame, Sacco and Vanzetti, and that assassinated the Rosenbergs." Here Nixon—previously unsuspected, for all his sins, to have been morally responsible for the execution of Sacco and Vanzetti—represents the American Evil, juxtaposed with a litany of martyrs (not coincidentally including two Italians who made the mistake of venturing to the United States).[51]

The legacy of the PCI's Manichaean view of the world continued into the 1980s, even though most party leaders and members by then took a more nuanced view of both the United States and the Soviet Union. Vilification of the United States remained an important feature of PCI discourse through its concluding national congress in 1991. The idealization of the Communist regimes, however, had sharply eroded by that time. A survey of delegates to that congress found that 93 percent agreed with the statement "The United States is an imperialist power," while a less robust 53 percent agreed with the statement "Despite everything, Eastern Europe has achieved important social advances."[52]

De-Stalinization

In 1956, Khrushchev's revelations about Stalin's Great Terror and about the huge dimensions of his illegal repression, and Khrushchev's denunciations of the cult of personality surrounding Stalin, delivered a blow to the PCI. Togliatti, on his return from the Twentieth Soviet Communist Party Congress where Khrushchev's secret speech was given, tried to keep the matter quiet, but word was eventually leaked to American newspapers and then picked up by the Italian press (although the Communist press never published it).[53] The PCI leaders feared that the entire symbolic edifice of the Soviet paradise and the world's Great Savior would collapse, bringing the party's credibility down along with it.

Togliatti met this threat with a twofold approach: (1) painting Stalin's misdeeds not as "crimes" but as "errors," the identification and correction of which were but further evidence of the vitality of the Soviet system; and (2) counterattacking, dismissing the criticisms of the USSR (and of the PCI's support for the USSR) as but a smoke screen cynically employed by the agents of capitalism and imperialism.

Shortly after the revelations had come to light, Togliatti explained their meaning to party activists at a meeting in Livorno. He first argued that the criticisms directed at Stalin could be properly seen only in the context of the dislocations inevitably produced by the October Revolution. The "errors that Stalin committed," he went on to say, occurred as unfortunate side effects of the great process of transforming Russian society: "To err is human, when one is embarking on a road no one has tread before." Not only had these errors not undermined the fundamental socialist content of the Soviet regime but, Togliatti assured his comrades, "it was inevitable that they would eventually be denounced and corrected, because they were in conflict with this content."[54]

In this interpretation of Stalin's "errors," whatever the mistakes were, they in no way sullied the reputations of the other heroic figures of the PCI pantheon. In a bit of historiographical revisionism, Gramsci and Togliatti were now transformed into early public critics of Stalin, while Marx, Engels, and Lenin remained above criticism, as befitting their saintly status.[55] As late as 1979, the official theses voted on by the PCI national congress blamed Stalin's "crimes" (by then the word could be used) largely on the "lack of socialist revolution in Western Europe" and dismissed as absurd the "thesis that the main cause should instead be assigned to the thought of Lenin, or indeed to Marx himself."[56]

This tactic was, for the most part, successful. Although the party lost a handful of nationally visible figures, very few party leaders defected, while the industrial workers and agricultural laborers who made up the backbone of the membership were remarkably unmoved by the revelations.[57] Togliatti could boast, eight years later: "Do you remember what happened then? Everyone thought that we were finished. . . . And instead nothing of the sort happened."[58] Indeed, in 1961, when Togliatti returned to Moscow for the Twenty-second Congress of the Soviet Communist Party, he reverentially carried a wreath to Stalin's tomb.[59]

Still, the revelations had an effect, and Stalin was gradually displaced from PCI sainthood. Typical of the erasure was a booklet on the history of the party, published by the PCI in connection with the upcoming Tenth Party Congress in 1964. The pages on the history of the PCI in the 1920s and 1930s nowhere mention Stalin's name (nor, for that matter, is the Hitler-Stalin pact mentioned). Indeed, the first reference to Stalin comes only in a later chapter on the "new party." There, in a somewhat roundabout way, the centrality of Gramsci to the party, as opposed to Stalin, is asserted:

> Gramsci's conceptions had already become, and would in the future continue to be . . . an essential element in how the conception of the *New Party* would develop. The conception of the New Party was elaborated and defined, in its essential elements, in terms of the war of Liberation immediately thereafter. In this process, it had to be subjected to severe critical review so that it would be in a position to advance rapidly ahead in light of the Twentieth Congress of the Soviet Communist Party (1956) and the criticisms of the methods used by the leadership in the Stalin period.[60]

Just what this critical self-examination consisted of, and how it changed the PCI, were left unspecified.

The end of the 1960s saw the PCI still committed to a heroic image of the Soviet Union, but by then the emphasis was less on the role of the USSR in the war—a topic difficult to discuss without mentioning Stalin—than on the symbolically safer October Revolution.

The mood had become defensive, and Soviet leaders were no longer glorified. The deeply rooted belief in the Soviet Union as Savior of the world had certainly eroded within the PCI by the end of the 1960s and suffered a further blow with the PCI's denunciation of the Soviet invasion of Czechoslovakia in 1968. Yet more than a little of the Savior imagery remained. In his address to the PCI national congress in 1969, for example, Berlinguer provided this view of history: "There is a historical, worldwide continuity from the October Revolution, and the construction of socialism in the Soviet Union, and continuing through the transformation—on a socialist basis—of other countries, on an international scale." Having established this link between the present USSR and the fabled October Revolution, Berlinguer went on to connect it with all that was good:

> This continuity—notwithstanding the contradictions and errors—is expressed not only in the structural transformations that have revolutionized more than half of humanity, but also, at the same time, in the role that the Soviet Union and the socialist countries have played in the struggle against imperialism, Fascism, and reaction, and in the struggle for peace, for national independence, for democracy and socialism. It is the recognition of this reality, of this function, that has led us to align ourselves always, in the anti-Fascist, democratic, and socialist struggle, on the side of the October Revolution.

Here Berlinguer is addressing, above all, the old guard of the party, who were disoriented by his recent criticism of the Soviet Union's actions in Czechoslovakia. He sought to comfort them by proclaiming, "For this reason we have always rejected and we continue to reject anti-Sovietism in all the forms in which it presents itself."[61]

By the late 1970s, any discussion of the Soviet Union and the other "socialist" states took on a dual character. Attempts were made to put more distance between the PCI and these regimes, yet the party's dichotomous worldview remained. The theses on the "socialist countries" approved by the national PCI congress in 1979 illustrate this approach. Again, they begin with the mythical October Revolution: "The October Revolution and the construction of a new society, in Russia and later in other countries, had the value of producing a historic break with the system of imperialism and capitalist exploitation, generating national and social revolutions." After paying further tribute to the many contributions these socialist states had made, the party thesis added the by-then-obligatory caveat: no, these societies were not perfect, indeed they had certain "limits, contradictions, and errors," especially "as far as democracy is concerned."[62] This rather murky antipodal position was restated, in more succinct form, a bit later in the document: "The paths followed by these societies constitute a patrimony of positive experiences, though afflicted by errors which any emancipatory force must recognize so that it can understand."[63] The question of just what the party patrimony consisted of, and who could claim its mantle, would lie at the heart of the fight over the future of the PCI a decade later.

chapter four

What's in a Name?

> Power comes through becoming
> authorized to provide a name for a thing, and thus
> to make it experienced in a new way.
>
> —Pierre Bourdieu, *Outline of a Theory of Practice*

For millions of Italians, from the end of the Second World War through the 1980s, personal identity was rooted in the Communist Party and its symbolism: "Sono comunista" (I am a Communist) was a statement not only of people's political allegiance but of their core identity. For many, being identified as Communist was more salient and more satisfying than being identified as Italian.

Party statutes expressed the all-encompassing social and moral nature of the Communist identity. The 1975 statute is typical in alerting members that other people viewed them as representatives of the party: "Each Communist Party member must understand that his fellow workers and students, his neighbors, his acquaintances and relatives all look on him as a combatant for a better world, for a more just and saner society." Accordingly, each member was urged to "constantly strive to set an example with his private life, with his treatment of his family, his neighbors, his fellow workers, setting an example of moral behavior, honesty, and a spirit of human and social solidarity."[1]

Providing people with such a unitary identity entailed constant symbolic work, primarily carried out at the local level. The party's goal was to provide a PCI section in every community throughout the country, as well as in all major factories and places of employment. These sections sponsored a host of activities rich in the display of the party's symbols, the telling of its sacred myths, and the performance of its sacred rites.[2] Through participation in this symbolic system, people who otherwise had little in common—neither education, nor class, nor even language—would be made to feel as if they shared a fundamental identity.[3]

At the height of its influence, in the mid-1970s, the PCI counted a third of all members of parliament, nearly as many as the Christian Democrats, and it headed the governments of all the nation's largest cities and many of its regions. By the beginning of the 1980s, however, optimism about the party's future began to erode, as both the PCI's percentage of the vote and its membership started to shrink. The decline began at a time when the nation's attention was riveted on the struggle being waged by members of the Red Brigades and allied groups, who unleashed a campaign of political terrorism that claimed the traditional symbols of Communism as their own. The PCI's opponents, seizing on this symbolism, sought to blame the "Communists" for the terrorist groups and their actions, while the PCI did all it could to discredit the claims made by these groups to what the party regarded as its own sacred symbols.[4]

This particular threat dwindled in the early 1980s when the police were finally able to crush the Red Brigades and related left-wing guerrilla groups. More ominous for the party leaders, however, were developments of the late 1980s in the Soviet Union and Eastern Europe, which threatened to undermine the allure of the party's Communist identity and to turn the party's traditional "fraternal" relations with the governments of the Communist countries and their ruling party apparatuses into an insufferable burden.

As Berliners began to dismantle their wall, and as Communist regimes throughout Europe crumbled, the party head, Achille Occhetto, having consulted secretly only with his closest allies among the party leaders, announced that the time had come to create a new party, with a new name. His announcement—referred to as the *svolta*—was a bombshell, enraging his opponents in the party leadership (who branded the move dictatorial and shameful) while leaving the mass of committed members in shock, their identity cast out, the myths to which they had been committed in jeopardy, and their sense of their own history threatened.

But above all else, the focus at the end of 1989, as these dramatic events began to unfold, was on the problem of the name.

The Magical Power of Naming

Pierre Bourdieu entreats us to pay more attention to the role played by words in the construction of social reality. Indeed, he argues that the social sciences "must take as their object of study the social operations of *naming* and the rites of institution through which they are accomplished".[5] We should not view the emergence of these objectifications as the mysterious result of some kind of anonymous social process. Rather, in Bourdieu's view, the battle over the power to name should be seen as a competition among elites.

Bourdieu refers to the leader's ability to provide a representation for a collectivity as "his truly magical power over the group" (192). In this, he echoes Stanley Tambiah's now classic discussion of the "magical power of words," which, in turn, builds on the theme developed earlier by Malinowski in his study of Trobriand magic.[6] As Tambiah observes, the notion that naming is a creative power, one that brings reality into being rather than simply provides a name for an already existing "thing," is found throughout the world and throughout history. Such a belief is often linked to a concept of supernatural beings who have the power, merely by uttering a name, to bring about the thing so named. The word, in short, is the breath of God; the word creates the world.

"By structuring the perception which social agents have of the social world," writes Bourdieu, "the act of naming helps to establish the structure of this world." No element in the quest for political power is more basic than the struggle over the right to name: "There is no social agent who does not aspire, as far as his circumstances permit, to have the power to name and to create the world through naming" (105). The same theme was dear to Michel Foucault as well, for Foucault viewed the ability to lock people into certain identities as the kernel of the exercise of power.[7]

The struggle over the future of the PCI in the months following the fall of the Berlin Wall offers a valuable vantage point for examining these processes. It allows us to consider the circumstances under which a political leader seizes the power to name and, by so naming, changes the world and changes the identity of those who follow him. It allows us to explore what Bourdieu refers to as the "alchemy of representation . . . through which the representative creates the group which creates him" (106).

The naming at stake here is of a crucial kind, for it involves the ability to provide people with a name for themselves, with a symbolic identity that links them both to their leader and to one another. The PCI struggle is also intriguing because the power holder in this case not only calls on people to take up a new name, and hence a new identity, but beseeches them to abandon their old name, and with it their previous identity.

To understand the nature of the process through which naming creates political reality, we need to understand the universe of named social-political groupings that already exists. For example, to understand what the social identity of Catholic means today in the United States, one has to know about the identity of Protestant, whereas in Italy in the 1950s one could not understand what a Catholic identity meant without knowing about the alternative identity of Communist. To provide a name for a group means not only to create a group and create an identity for individuals identifying with it but also to provide a contrast between those in the group and those outside it.

Under certain circumstances, including those discussed here, the divisions of society brought about by naming have another dimension. The new name not only distinguishes one's own group from others, and thus provides the individual with a basis for social identity, but also distinguishes between that which is sacred and that which is profane.[8]

What follows, then, is an investigation of just how leaders manipulate symbols and use their symbolic capital to provide people with new representations of themselves. Various obstacles hinder the accomplishment of such "symbolic violence," as Bourdieu has called this process. Two are of particular interest: (1) the reluctance of the mass of the "represented" to give up their old name and, thus, their old identity; and (2) the opposition posed by other members of the political elite, who clamor to become the "representers." The power of these competing elites depends on their ability to discredit the renaming efforts of their rivals and to substitute themselves as authors of any re-representation.

Abandoning a Name

In announcing the svolta, party leader Achille Occhetto chose not to propose a new name, calling instead—rather hazily—for a "fase costituente," which would lead to a "new political formation." This new political formation would, Occhetto hoped, encompass not only the old PCI but also a variety of organized and unorganized groups on the Left.

Occhetto's wisdom in proposing that party members give up their old name, their old identity, without offering a new one to take its place is worth considering. The case illustrates the limits on a political leader's power to name. To immediately propose a new name risked provoking a trauma too great for party members to endure. The new symbolism would have to be negotiated in a longer process, involving complex semiotic and political considerations.

Most notable among these was the need to take into account the symbolism being used by the PCI's competitors.[9] Decades of glorifying the identity of Communist had meant unceasing PCI efforts to discredit alternative symbolism in the political arena, most notably the symbols associated with the Socialists and the Social Democrats. To embrace such symbolism overnight was unthinkable.

Yet the power of naming is the power of calling the world into existence, and this is just what Occhetto did, even without providing a new name for the party (indeed, even without initially acknowledging that the new entity would be a party at all). The nameless *nuova formazione* soon acquired the (epistemologically) paradoxical name of the *cosa*—the "thing"—following Occhetto's proclamation: "First comes the thing and then the name" (Prima viene la cosa e poi il nome).[10]

This famous phrase became part of the symbolic battle Occhetto was waging, yet his actions show the fallacy—if not the duplicity—of his claim. What came first was in fact the name: it was Occhetto's announcement that the name of the party would be changed, and that—though at the time he preferred to express himself only indirectly on this issue—the party would no longer be called Communist, that in itself remade the political scene. Indeed, it was clearly a case of first the name, and then the thing. A number of observers of the Italian political scene have argued that had Occhetto simply gone ahead with all his substantive policy and organizational changes without proposing to change the party's name, there would have been no major crisis in the party, and the huge amount of suffering by party members would have been avoided.[11] What was most important was the name: the importance of not being Communist.

This point became a major weapon of the splinter group, the Rifondazione comunista, created by PCI leaders who refused to join the party majority in abandoning the Communist name. This group would, in the wake of the Twentieth PCI Congress, which gave rise to the PDS, break off from the parent party and establish its own, Communist party. Although the philo-Soviet stalwart Armando Cossutta was at the center of this group, it included quite different segments of the old PCI as well, from left-wing union leaders to a faction identified with the old Manifesto movement, veterans of earlier campaigns for increased democracy within the PCI.

Organized around the emotional cry that they would never renounce their identity as Communist, the group, somewhat ironically, turned to the Italian court system to legitimate their use of the old party name (Partito comunista italiano). In justifying their right to do so, and their claim that the new no-longer-Communist party, the PDS, had given up its right to the old name, they argued, "For quite a long time in fact the new political formation came to be officially labeled 'the Thing,' where the very vagueness of the name served to indicate the broad universe of possible names, which excluded only that of *Communist*."[12]

In proposing the elimination of the old name, Occhetto faced a plenitude of problems, for the party had spent decades elaborating a symbolic, mythic, and ritual system glorifying the name of Communist. What bound the members to one another, and what bound them to the party leaders, was just this representation. Those who would "besmirch" the name were guilty not simply of political opposition but of sacrilege.

Given these pressures, Occhetto proposed jettisoning the name without directly calling the sacred symbolism into question. He denied that his proposal was the result of any need to distance the party from events in Eastern Europe, asserting that the PCI had had absolutely nothing to do with the repressive regimes and parties in that part of the world.[13] Yet, of course, the PCI had a great deal to do with them, sharing with them a name and a universe of symbolism, rites, and myths.

This point is nicely made in a poignant vignette published in *L'Unità*, describing the anguish that an elderly PCI member experienced while watching televised reports of the massacre of Tiananmen Square. Practically in tears, he asked his younger friend, "Why, wherever we come to power, do such things happen?" What is revealing is the man's use of "we," his sense of identity with the Communists in China. It is a sense of solidarity produced, above all, by sharing a name, and with that name a panoply of symbols. It was just this symbolic equivalence that Occhetto sought to erase.[14]

Occhetto, although ironically helped by the PCI's traditions of endowing its party leader with charisma and viewing the secretary as the embodiment of the party, faced vigorous opposition both from party members and from segments of the party leadership. He recognized the emotional potency of the Communist identity in the gradual manner in which he moved away from the Communist identification. Asked in December 1989 how he would define himself after the new party was formed, for example, he responded, "I am and I remain an Italian Communist." In this he allied himself with the tens of thousands who in section meetings and in letters to the editor of the PCI press proudly and firmly stated they would call themselves Communist until the day they died (indeed, even after, given the tradition of draping the flag of the party section over the casket of deceased militants).[15] He continued to sprinkle his speeches to party members with the phrase *noi comunisti* (we Communists), but this practice would not last long.

At this stage of the transition, Occhetto argued that, in giving up the Communist name and in giving birth to a new political entity in which other forces would join them, the Communists would be enlarging and strengthening their political base. Although this was no doubt Occhetto's ambition, what the PCI leader did not say was that it was necessary to unburden the party of symbolism that had become irremediably tarnished. The adoption of a new set of symbols not only would cause others to view the "Communists" differently but would cause the old members to view themselves differently as well. It was a move that had the additional virtue of marginalizing his opponents within the party leadership, as they would inevitably rally around the (now oppositional) Communist symbolism.

Yet these goals could not be directly expressed; indeed, they had to be repudiated. The identity of the members could not be directly attacked; their self-conception could only gradually be changed.

At the heart of the matter was, again, the relation of the name to the thing. The opposition never tired of denouncing Occhetto for proposing the *scioglimento* (dissolution) or the *liquidazione* of the party, a charge the party secretary angrily and repeatedly denied. Such dissolution or liquidation would mean, of course, the liquidation of the identity of the huge number of people who identified with the PCI.

Communist as Identity

Selfhood is problematic: the self must be constructed by weaving together available symbols, and it must be constantly shored up.[16] As James Fernandez puts it, "We need to become objects to ourselves." It was Abner Cohen's great insight to see that for most people this process of objectification takes place through symbols offered to them by various interest groups. Such interest groups, he argues, "always attempt to manipulate and structure the selves of their members to further their own ends." True, people are themselves creative agents, and may accept, modify, or reject such manipulations. But, for the most part, people seeking a stable sense of self are attracted to the symbols of personal identity provided by elites. Cohen declares, "As our subjective life is shifting, vague and chaotic, we are only too happy to be assisted by the objective symbolic formulations provided to us by 'experts.'"[17]

"Words wreak havoc," wrote Sartre, "when they find a name for what had up to then been lived namelessly."[18] The havoc that Occhetto's announcement wreaked among the membership of the PCI was, curiously, caused by their sudden discovery that they no longer had a name. They were told that their old name would not do, yet this name had provided them with their identity, their means of objectifying themselves to themselves.

Many members reacted with severe distress to the prospect of being deprived of their name. Despite attempts by Occhetto and his allies to assure the membership that the name and symbol of the party were not so important, the name and symbol were all that many members wanted to talk about. As one Central Committee member wrote in the immediate aftermath of Occhetto's announcement, speaking of the panic among comrades in his factory, "There are strong fears of a loss of identity." In this and many other cases, loss of identity had a double reference, referring to both the identity of the party and the identity of the individual.[19]

Another member reflected on just what being able to call oneself a Communist meant:

> Being a communist in Italy represented for entire generations a clear, direct, emotional expression of recognition, the expression of a strong identity that in a single word brought together ideas, plans, hopes, delusions, and suffering. To call yourself Communist is to recognize yourself as one among the others. . . . This is the pride of being Communist, and it should be no surprise today that throughout the membership people are upset, preoccupied, and angry. Those who do not take this into account beware.[20]

In a working-class neighborhood in Palermo, where the Communists had always been an embattled minority, older party members expressed outrage over the proposed name change. As the local section head stated, "The old folks, the old militants who were raised in the postwar years, continue to experience as pure agony what they define as 'the abandonment of our reason for being.'"[21]

When the dissident faction of the PCI leadership decided to found a still-Communist party, they were able to count on the loyalty produced by this sort of representation. In September 1990, they organized a national assembly of PCI forces opposed to the name change. A journalist described the mood: " 'No one can take the adjective "Communist" away from us' is the unanimous comment of all those who attended." Reflecting the general sentiment, one of the elderly activists in attendance declared, "I have nothing to repent, nothing to feel guilty about, I don't understand then why I have to stop calling myself Communist." And another, who arrived at the meeting carrying a red flag, complete with a sculpted hammer and sickle on the top, explained, "I will carry this flag to my grave, because I want to die a Communist."[22]

The deep fervor with which many identified with the party, and the sacredness that the party's symbols—first among these, the party name—had for them, lead inevitably to a comparison with religion. Although party ideology long rejected this comparison—a rejection motivated not only by Marxist views of religion but also by the PCI's interest in attracting Catholics to the party—many members drew this parallel. As one Central Committee member described the distress produced by Occhetto's recent announcement of the svolta: "The fact is that for each of us Communism was not just a party, it was first of all a grand idea and ideology, a little like Christianity was and still is today. What is to us basically like a church tears at us with the thought that we are abandoning, betraying our own 'Christ/Marx.'"[23] Likewise, Nilde Jotti, one of the party's most prominent leaders, reflected on the crisis overtaking the party when, in May 1990, she declared, "It's as if the pope were to say that Christ never existed."[24]

In the effort to save their Communist identity, members wrestled with semantics. They desperately sought to define *Communist* in such a way as to exclude the associations that the term had for almost everyone around them. In party sections throughout the country, and at every level of the party bureaucracy, PCI members argued that they were the only real Communists; those in the Soviet Union, in China, in Rumania were impostors. As one party member from Turin said, "The Eastern regimes that are crumbling were never Communist regimes . . . there isn't even a crumb of Communism in them. So we don't feel so responsible for them that we should change our name." The religious quality of her commitment to the Communist name is even clearer in her account of how, the previous year, just before the death of her father, a "faithful, old Communist," she told him of the imminent collapse of the Soviet regime. He responded, she said, "vehemently: 'The Soviet regime will crumble, but Communism never!' "[25]

The magical value of the name was reflected in the anguished comments of party members from throughout the country. It was bad enough to touch the other sacred symbolism of the party, but the name was holy above all, for it had a double nature: the name of the party served also as the name of the member. Ones Maini, a forty-four-year-old bus driver, who was interviewed while helping out with the decorations at a local PCI festival, put it this way: "Go ahead and change the symbol, use a rose or whatever you like. While I was hoisting the red flags it occurred to me that maybe this will be the last time that we use them. *Pazienza!* But the name is another story." He concluded, "If you like, you could add something to what is already there. It could be called the Democratic Communist Party." The journalist who interviewed him observed, "Add, revise, cut, just as long you save that word, which, for Ones Maini, is sacred."[26]

The power of the word *Communist* was such that it was thought to offer talismanic protection to those who invoked it. Consider the view of an auto worker, expressed in his address to the party's Central Committee following the announcement of the svolta: "The fear that, without the word *Communist,* the workers will feel themselves weakened and more exposed to the capitalist offensive is fully justified."[27] Indeed, members angered by the proposed name change often argued that society "needs us Communists."[28] Again, the relation between the change of the name and the change of the thing should give us pause for reflection. A strong identity was being abandoned for one that remained wholly to define. As one of the leaders of the opposition protested, "We risk being neither fish nor fowl."[29]

The relation between the name and the thing troubled the members and was a theme constantly stressed by leaders of the opposition. Occhetto continued to argue first the thing and then the name, although he operated in precisely the opposite way. For the opposition, it was the name that presented the greatest guarantee of the thing. The remarks of Livia Turco, one of the highest-ranking women in the party, reflect these concerns. "There is a relation," she said, "between things and their name," and she continued, "Today, our identity, our position as Communists, is more guaranteed by a name, by its idealistic and even ideological associations, than it is by any program or policies." She concluded, "Being Communist is more a matter of belonging than a critical program of action or a movement."[30]

In the months of debate, among those most anguished about the problem of the name and personal identity were the *donne comuniste* (women Communists). These were women who had organized their own caucus within the party and for whom the double identity—women and Communist—afforded both personal and political symbolic capital. The prospect of no longer being able to refer to themselves as donne comuniste, along with the apparent absence of any new, comparable identity, produced intense unease.[31]

The members of the women's caucus were among those who most clearly saw the centrality of the name to the thing. One of them argued, immediately following Occhetto's 1989 announcement, "My political experience as a woman tells me that, to put a group together, you must first make yourself identifiable." She concluded that "resolving the question of the name is not a problem that comes later, not something that is in itself of little importance. It concerns the political substance of the proposal because it is the only concrete indication that we give of ourselves."[32]

One of the intriguing themes to emerge in the debate over the PCI's name was the importance of defending the party's "honor." Those opposed to the name change defined their struggle as that of defending the honor of the Communist name, and no phrase was more commonly uttered by those opposing the change than "We have no reason to be ashamed of ourselves." Accompanying this proud assertion came, inevitably, the further argument that it was the Communist parties of the East and not the PCI who had dishonored the Communist name ("disonorato il nome del comunismo").[33] The opponents of the name change repeatedly accused

Occhetto of casting aspersions on the *onorabilità* of the name.[34] Defensively, Occhetto's allies felt the need to assure party members that the PCI enjoyed, in the words of Piero Fassino, an "honored name," of which they had "no reason to be ashamed."[35]

The battle over the party's honor reveals something quite important: the symbolic equivalence drawn between the name of the party and the (family) name of the person. Just as one must defend one's family name from dishonor, so must one defend one's party name. Significantly, the extension of this kind of identification from family to party marked no other political party in Italy. No one was concerned with upholding the honor of the name *Christian Democrat*, nor did the spectacular fall in 1993 of the Socialist Party lead to any notable popular concern about the honor associated with the name *Socialist*.

Occhetto's efforts to change the name of the PCI, and thereby to change its nature, represent a clear instance of what Bourdieu calls the exercise of political power through the promulgation of "authorized language." Although Occhetto was the duly elected party head, in this case he wielded what Bourdieu refers to as "heretical power." In Bourdieu's terms, he possessed the "strength of the sorcerer." Although he was the high priest of the PCI, Occhetto was very much engaged in heresy, in the desecration—or the desacralization—of the most holy symbolism of his own party. The magic he performed consisted of the objectification of "unformulated experiences." He sought, in short, to create a new symbol that would alter people's perceptions not only of the party but of themselves.[36]

Although the power to name is arguably the greatest of all powers—redefining reality and the social world—part of the magic of naming comes from the ability to portray the new name not as a creation of the magician but, rather, as somehow a reflection of the very nature of things. While the leader may create his or her following through the creative act of naming, the followers must be led to believe that some higher power created their name and hence produced their leader. This higher power may be conceived in otherworldly form, but in the political sphere these days—at least in the West—it is likely to be viewed in a more down-to-earth fashion as the expression of the general will.

Occhetto sought to convince members that the decision to change the party's name was in fact being made by them and not by him. In particular, he had to deny the insistent charge by his opponents within the party that he had not only decided to liquidate the Communist name but had done so to appease those outside the party.

At the November 1989 meeting at which Occhetto first presented the svolta to the Central Committee, he framed the matter in a revealingly defensive and elliptical way: "If a party, in the face of events that alter the whole, complex political scene, were to decide of its own free will and without external pressure, to create, together with others, a new political formation, then yes, this would be something serious, something that would offend neither the rationale nor the honor of a political organization."[37]

Occhetto needed to give the impression that the members were creating him as the head of a new party, rather than he creating them. The terms *liquidation* and *dissolution* of the Communist party, used by his opponents, tapped into members' fear of loss of identity, of leaping into the void. In defense, Occhetto and his allies—not without leaving themselves open to occasional ridicule—introduced the term *autosuperamento* (literally, surpassing oneself, or emerging from oneself) to refer to the wholly autochthonous and transformative nature of the change being proposed.[38] Legitimacy could only come from within, and the putative source of that legitimacy could not be the leader; it had to be the party members.

Communists in Court: Suing over a Name

As the time approached for the Twentieth National PCI Congress—the congress designed to give birth to the new party's name (note, not the party's new name)—Occhetto planned a news conference to unveil the new name and symbol. The scene was reminiscent of the selection of a new pope, replete with the highly secret deliberations of the powerful, and the impatient and emotionally charged vigil of the represented. For Occhetto, what was crucial was to overcome the strident denunciations of the competing party elite and, at the same time, to assuage the anguish of the tens of thousands of members whose identity was emotionally bound up in the Communist name. The new name, the new representation, would have to excise the Communist label. Yet, Occhetto had to forestall the appropriation of the party symbolism by opposition groups. Around the same time, Occhetto's most implacable foes in the party began to plan secession, arguing that they wanted to remain in a party where they could continue, with pride, to call themselves Communist.

This prospect, which Occhetto had foreseen, haunted the PCI leader. The strength of the opposition was closely linked to the symbolic strength of the Communist name and the emotions produced by the name and its accompanying symbolism. What Occhetto feared most of all was that his opponents would claim the name as their own, that is, attempt to steal the symbolic capital of the PCI. This is exactly what happened.

Indeed, it happened in a way that neatly paralleled Occhetto's own strategy of autosuperamento. The leaders of the move to launch this new Communist organization presented themselves not as the creators of a Communist Party but, rather, as witnesses to a process of nature. In his harshly worded speech at the Twentieth PCI Congress in January 1991, the godfather of the new Communist Party, Armando Cossutta, proclaimed: "The need to feel and to be a Communist cannot be minimized and blotted out by acts of force. The Communist question exists. You must not, you cannot erase it. Driven from its names and its symbols, purged from all behavior, it would nonetheless arise again." Cossutta went on to argue that it was not he who wanted a split in the party—not he who was trespassing against the party's sacred solidarity—but rather the others: "You cannot prevent me from remaining a Communist, from thinking and acting as a Communist. Nor can you stop our children."[39]

"In the symbolic domain," writes Bourdieu, "takeovers by force appear as *takeovers of form*."[40] The minority struggled against the imposition of a new name and, with it, a new system of power. What remained crucial for them was *to remain Communist*, but what did this mean? By most traditional measures, there was little Communist ideological content to the PCI. The party embraced multiparty parliamentary government and opposed both nationalization of the nation's economy and democratic centralism. What was Communist about the party was above all its name and a variety of symbols, myths, and rites that went with it. This is what the party members had in common.

Occhetto and his allies, in their efforts to prevent the opposition from claiming the old party name and symbolism, were presented with some ticklish problems. If the new party was not a Communist party, if it was going to be something entirely new, how could it claim symbolic continuity with its past? How, in particular, could it prevent others from adopting the old Communist name and symbolism? Combating the attempts of others to occupy the old symbolic space vacated by the PCI risked undermining the new party's claim to being new.

Tellingly, Occhetto, while insisting on changing the name of the party, was willing to compromise in other aspects of the symbolic domain. He retained much of the old party symbolism, including the red flags, the old party songs, the incessant use of *comrade* (*compagno*) in ritualized speech, and the party festivals, still called *feste dell'Unità*. Only the hammer and sickle, though never directly spurned, came to be seen as too closely allied with the Communist identity to be displayed any more than necessary. The other symbols were slowly redefined to be interpreted not as Communist but as part of a more generic socialist heritage.

In October 1990, Occhetto announced the new name, and a composite symbol. The name, Partito democratico della sinistra

(Democratic Party of the Left), could hardly have been more generic, rejecting not only the Communist label but also the Socialist and Social Democratic ones. The name merely provided a symbolic place-marker, locating the party on the Left. Indeed, the relational value of the new name was such that one member indignantly replied to the announcement by muttering, "as if the PCI weren't democratic!"

The new symbol was dominated by a powerful oak tree, composed of a sturdy trunk and abundant green leaves. Although attempts were made to portray the tree as a traditional symbol of the Left (much being made of the symbolic use of the tree in the French Revolution), it lacked any such emotional or cognitive resonance for most people. The symbol contrasted sharply with the old one, which had been dominated by the red flag and the hammer and sickle. Yet, cleverly, a small addition was made to the design: at the base of the tree, where the roots grew, lay the old party emblem, complete with flags, hammer and sickle, and the letters "PCI."[41]

The importance of this political maneuver would soon become clear. The setting for the first important battle over the new name—a Roman court—offered an ironic source of authorization for determining who could legitimately call themselves Communist. Indeed, within days of the majority vote at the Twentieth—and presumably last—Congress of the PCI, which gave rise to the PDS, a secessionist group submitted a formal petition to the Tribunale di Roma. The purpose of the petition was to receive court authorization for the group to use, as its name, Partito comunista italiano.

The suit rested on the argument that there existed—in the political universe—a Communist ideology, formerly represented by the PCI but now repudiated by it with the formation of the PDS:

> If a party is formed with the goal of advancing a national politics in a strictly Communist direction, you cannot prevent such a party from identifying itself with the name and the symbols of the Communist tradition. Still less can the exercise of such a

right . . . be prevented by another political group that, like the current PDS, has voluntarily jettisoned the signs that it had formerly possessed, claiming that they no longer correspond to its current political-ideological patrimony and, in the end, that they did not at all reflect its personal identity.[42]

The argument employed here is revealing in several ways, not least of which is its explicit equation of "personal identity" with the identity of a political representation. It is also revealing in its clear commitment to the theory of first the thing and then the name. The new party, the suit argues, deserves the name Partito comunista italiano because that is what it is.

In their heated reply to the court, lawyers for the PDS rejected the secessionist group's arguments. They claimed the exclusive right to the symbolism of the "PCI" without going so far as to argue that the PDS was still a "Communist" party. Occhetto's agents contended, "The use of the name and the symbols of the Italian Communist Party . . . clearly constitute the main instrument and vehicle through which the newly constituted association makes known its existence and attempts to extend its influence." In short, the threat represented by the nascent party lay in neither its program nor its ideology nor its leadership but in its attempt to appropriate the name and related symbols of the old PCI.[43]

At the core of the PDS's defense was its claim to symbolic continuity, that it "retains the symbol and the initials [of the PCI] in its new emblem, and does so because it constitutes the natural continuation of the PCI experience."[44] The argument was over symbolic representations. In their legal brief, the PDS lawyers expressed their horror over the secessionist party's recently announced membership card, which consisted of the name and symbol of the PCI, along with the dates "1921/1991." Clearly, the secessionist party sought to lay claim thereby to the symbolic identity of the old PCI, which had been founded in 1921.[45]

In responding to the secessionist party's petition, the PDS referred to it as the "self-named Italian Communist Party" (*autode-*

nominatesi Partito comunista italiano), a phrase that drew the ire of the leaders of the still-proud-to-be-Communist party. They attacked the PDS brief in these terms: "We do not, in particular, understand their reasoning in insisting on the fact that this association has been *self*-named the Italian Communist Party, as if this were not in the very nature of voluntary associations, and almost as if the name of the Democratic Party of the Left had somehow been bestowed on them by a decree of the President of the Republic!"[46]

In the end, the court sided with the PDS, citing the significance of the PDS's decision to retain the old emblem and name in its new symbol. The secessionist party was hence forbidden from using the name and emblem of the old party.[47] Occhetto's relief, however, was tempered by the realization that his success rested on an equivocation. The PDS was defined by its past, yet it was its past that Occhetto and his allies were most in need of escaping.

chapter five

Battling over the
Past to Change the Future

Truth is a thing of this world: it is produced only
by virtue of multiple forms of constraint.
—Michel Foucault, *Power/Knowledge*

Chi non ha memoria non ha futuro. (Those who
have no memory have no future.)
—Banner displayed at a demonstration of
the Jewish Youth Federation

We possess no other life, no other living sap, than
the treasures stored up from the past and digested,
assimilated, and created afresh by us.
—Simone Weil, *The Need for Roots*

Where God is dead, history reigns. When supernatural justifications
for holding power fail to persuade, history fills the void. Indeed, history
is the proving grounds for both religion and politics. The claims
to legitimacy of religion and politics are based on the construction
of historical narratives, the manufacture of events and heroes located
in the past. Battles for power in the present are fought by producing

alternative accounts of the past and alternative readings of its meaning.

The struggle for power is the struggle to tame the past, to seize it, to make it both intelligible and useful by objectifying it, by simplifying it. The invention of a future thus presupposes the invention of a past. In this light, the paradox of the dual meaning of "making history"—meaning "making a future" as well as "making a past"—dissolves.[1]

Just how and why the making of the past is so crucial to current political battles is a subject I shed light on by looking at the transformation of the PCI in 1989–91. Casting off the PCI's core identity as a *Communist* party, and constructing its new, post-Communist identity, entailed a battle over the past. Indeed, the forces arrayed for and against the move struggled mightily over the party's history. Future success depended on successful definition of the past, and the amount of political capital held by each side in the struggle varied with its ability to appropriate the past—through a process of reification and iconization—and make it usable.

There is some irony in critiquing the Italian Communist Party from the vantage point of the political uses of history, for one of the most influential intellectual forbears for the study of the politics of history is Antonio Gramsci, himself the principal icon in the historical pantheon of the PCI.[2] He saw that power stems not so much from physical coercion as from symbolic production. The scholars who today are drawn to the question of how rule is accomplished commonly cite the influence of Gramsci's work on hegemony.[3]

Anthropologist Ana Alonso, for example, makes the link between history and hegemony in this way: "If social action is mediated by history, it is because the past has a political and discursive significance. Memory, meaning, and power are internally related." She concludes, "Thus, an inquiry into the construction and dissemination of historical memory, itself a central site for the production of effects of power, is critical for an analysis of hegemony."[4]

But just how does this struggle take place? What means are used to tame the past and mobilize it to serve present political ends? And why, after all, is the past so precious to us? The factional strife in the PCI offers an instructive vantage point from which to pursue these questions. In doing so, I identify four processes that help provide answers: (1) the objectification of history, (2) the sacralization of history, (3) the political construction of the self through history, and (4) the endowment of history with a narrative structure.

The Objectification of History

A political organization, like any other kind of organization, can be seen only through its symbolism.[5] Some of this symbolism is iconic—a party flag or mascot, for example—but much of it entails the direct symbolization of history.[6] The present is possible only through representation of the past.

Bronislaw Malinowski pioneered the anthropological study of the ways that people produce a history to justify their political position in the present—or to assert a claim to a position of power that they do not yet enjoy. For example, the assertion—through myth— that a group's ancestors rose out of the ground where the group now lives lends legitimacy to its claims to rule over all those who live there now. To take another example, anthropologist John Middleton found that the political rivalries among Lugbara elders, in what is now Uganda, were traditionally waged through conflicts over whose ancestors owned the sacred shrines and their associated ritual. Such claims are not by any means limited to small-scale or defunct societies, as the many nationalist struggles in the world today make clear. Wars would not be possible without an active program of symbolic production, and this production largely consists of the manufacture of rival histories.[7]

The contending factions of the PCI in 1989–91 fought on a battleground rich in historical symbolism. The trick for each side was to expropriate as much of the powerful symbolism as possible, while redefining the symbols' meaning to suit its goals. The combatants had to take special care in handling the symbols, for they were infused with an aura of sacrality. Mishandling them could lead to charges of sacrilege.

There was no more significant—or revealing—example of the objectification of history in the Communist Party struggle than the constant efforts by all sides to invoke the party's *patrimonio* (its patrimony, or heritage). Whether Achille Occhetto sought to reject the party's patrimony became a topic of intense debate. Of what did this precious patrimony consist? In the words of one official who was anxious about Occhetto's proposal, it was composed of "struggles, sacrifices, conquests, ideas, and values that are still valid today."[8]

The tightrope that Occhetto had to walk in dealing with this sacred patrimonio was evident in his concluding remarks to the stormy Nineteenth Party Congress, held in March 1990, where a divided party first approved his plan. Taking up the symbolism of honor and shame, he spoke of "the challenge of a force that wants to change not because it denies its own patrimony but because thanks to that experience and to that patrimony it is able to properly interpret the signs of a world that is changing."[9] Yet, despite such protestations, he continued to face accusations of denying the party's patrimony; he stood charged, in short, with denying the party's past.

The objectification of the past in the form of the party's patrimonio was also an issue in the suit filed by the secessionist Rifondazione comunista, following the Twentieth (and final) PCI Congress in early 1991. The suit, aimed at appropriating the PCI's name and symbol, was fought over the terrain of history, as shown by the legal brief of the Rifondazione comunista, countering that of the newly formed PDS. "The PDS. claims," the brief declared, "that the historical experience and the ideological patrimony that the Italian Communists accumulated from 1921 to 1991 'belong solely and exclusively to the PDS and constitute the roots of its existence.'" The Rifondazione comunista challenged this assertion, arguing that "*the so-called political and ideological patrimony* is not something that can belong exclusively to anyone." Its argument thus directly engaged the question of the reification of symbols and the objectification of patrimony: "Not only in fact are we not dealing in our civil code with *goods* that can be the object of ownership, but even if one were to view them absurdly as *things*, they would be of the category of *res communes omnium* and not be the exclusive property of anyone."[10]

The position taken by the lawyers for the neo-Communist splinter party was more than a little disingenuous. Their stance was based on discrediting the PDS's position that the party's patrimony was a "thing" that could be owned. Yet their objection was clearly tactical rather than epistemological. Indeed, in their own earlier battles within the PCI, these same pro-Communist leaders treated the patrimony of the party in exactly these reified terms. In their efforts to organize the still-proud-to-be-Communist party they would do all they could to establish their own exclusive claim to this patrimony.

The neo-Communist party's objectification of the PCI's patrimony in a form suitable for political exploitation was on display in the legal dispute. One of the bases for the PDS's defense was, in fact, the design of the new party's membership card. The neo-Communist party had lost no time in reproducing on its inaugural membership card the old symbol of the PCI, together with the dates 1921–91, providing an iconic embodiment of its claim to be the legitimate and historically continuous incarnation of the old PCI. The PDS countered that the PCI patrimony was its own exclusive property:

> With the membership campaign conducted, both emblematically and programmatically, under the insignias of the Italian Communist Party, the result over time will clearly be the increasing feeling among the public not only and not so much of (in itself a highly damaging) uncertainty, but indeed the conviction that, alongside a new political group constituted by the PDS, there exists *the* Italian Communist Party, proprietor of the historical experience and the patrimony of ideals (1921–91) contained in the symbol that it has adopted. Yet, we repeat,

that historical experience and that patrimony of ideals are the exclusive property of the PDS and constitute the roots of its existence.[11]

Opponents of the svolta, in harping on Occhetto's nefarious desire to liquidate the PCI, linked this action in the present to the "summary liquidation of the past."[12] Indeed, they made rueful comparison to a liquidation sale. As one complained, "We are witnessing . . . the selling off of our historical patrimony."[13] In this view, the patrimonio was something that had been "accumulated" at great cost.[14] One member wrote, indignantly, in a letter to the party paper, "The Communist name, in Italy, is not a name to be ashamed of; it has a history and a past that cannot be erased with a wipe of the sponge, replaced with a new dress."[15] Another, protesting directly to Occhetto, wrote, "Not only do you want to cancel these symbols, but you also want to cancel a history spanning over a half a century. . . . it is as though you were ashamed of being Communist. How can you erase . . . the glorious history of the most famous political party in the whole world?"[16]

The fear that the party's patrimonio was being liquidated was tied, for many members opposed to the svolta, to the fear that their history was being redefined. Nothing hit this nerve more quickly than ritual and iconic portrayals of that history, for it was through such representations that the historical patrimony could be touched, made real.

For many of the older compagni, the membership card itself had acquired a sacred aura, linking them to a mythic past, making the symbolism palpable. A sixty-year-old woman from Ferrara, who had joined the PCI at age eighteen, proudly proclaimed, "I have kept all my membership cards, and I will always keep them." Given this attitude, it is not hard to see why the PDS leaders reacted so strongly to the membership card of the neo-Communist splinter.

The role of the icon in defining history, and thereby defining the present, was similarly evident in another episode, prompted by an irate letter sent to *L'Unità*. The letter writer vehemently attacked the symbolic content of the PCI membership card that had been issued right after the svolta had been approved (but before the PDS had been formed). The letter is worth quoting in full:

> Dear *L'Unità*, my first PCI membership card bears the date I joined: April 24, 1945.[17] I have just read in the Friday insert of *l'Unità* . . . that next year's membership card will have the inscription "PCI 1946–1991. From the Resistance to the future." Let me first say that I am, though with mixed feelings, in favor of motion one, and for me the new proposed symbol is fine. I'm happy to have the inscription "PCI" on the new membership card, but I can't understand that "1946." Why this confusion of dates? (Forty-fifth anniversary of the new Republic? The Resistance in 1946?) I myself took part, in a very modest way, in the Resistance, but it was a little before '46, and I have been a member since '45. Why do you want to take a year away from me?
>
> I already had some uncertainty about what kind of party was being prepared for me for the future; but do they really want to erase a large part of our tradition? Then why not provide personalized membership cards, as they do in the USA with car license plates? And all this coming on our seventieth anniversary from 1921!
>
> I plan to take out my forty-seventh membership card only if it contains the dates April 24, 1945–January 1, 1991.[18]

The letter shows, first, some implications of one of the familiar aspects of the objectification of time: the celebration of anniversaries on a decennial (or, in this case, every-five-year) basis, privileging certain bundles of time over others. But it also points to another aspect, dear to the hearts of structuralists, for what is so striking about the party's choice of celebrating 1991 as the forty-fifth anniversary of the founding of the postwar Republic is what was *not* iconically celebrated: the seventieth anniversary of the founding of the PCI. Rather, it was the neo-Communist splinter party that sought to give tangible form to this historical identification through its first membership cards.

Piero Fassino, one of the leaders of the PCI, took this objectification of time a step further, giving time itself as a reason for leaving Communism behind. He explained, "Communism as a concrete political experience and form of state organization belongs to the twentieth century—that is, to a century about to end—and it would be difficult for it to belong to the new century, which we are about to enter."[19] Time is thus reified and divided into manageable chunks. Centuries, like books, come to an end.

The Sacralization of History

The past is sacred. The high priests of politics not only must be adept in manipulating the powerful symbols of the present but also must know how to define a past. In this, of course, they are no different from the prophets and priests of religion, whose power derives from a particular view of the past, and whose disputes in the present typically involve conflicting interpretations of what happened long ago.

In dealing with the uncomfortable similarities between the histories constructed by historians and those constructed by leaders of religious movements, scholars have often resorted to a distinction made between history and myth. In his book *Political Myth*, for example, Henry Tudor cautions us not to confuse myth with history, warning us that "much that passes for history is properly speaking myth." The key distinction, according to Tudor, concerns the grounds for believing the narrative to be true. In the case of history, veracity is judged on the basis of the use of relevant evidence and the consistency of the argument "with other conclusions reached concerning the same period or sequence of events." By contrast, the "myth-maker proceeds in a different fashion altogether." The aim of myth, as opposed to history, in this view, is practical. It seeks "either to advocate a certain course of action or to justify acceptance of an existing state of affairs." People believe myths to be true, then, "not because the historical evidence is compelling, but because they make sense of [their] present existence." The selection of the events that are included in the myth is based partly on what people "think ought to have happened, and partly because they are consistent with the drama as a whole."[20]

It follows from this view that the circumstances leading to a change in historical understanding differ between history and myth. The mythmaker reshapes accounts of the past, Tudor argues, when a "change in his circumstances has brought about a corresponding change in his practical position." By contrast, the historian alters accounts of the past only when provoked to do so by the emergence of new evidence or "because he considers previous accounts to be based on an incorrect interpretation of the existing evidence." Tudor concludes, "Where the historian deploys current knowledge in an attempt to elucidate the past, the myth-maker does so in order to make a point of practical importance to his contemporaries. And between the two there is a world of difference."[21]

But is there really such a great difference? What forces lead historians to conclude that current interpretations of the past are erroneous? What impels them to locate new evidence? What prompts them to seize on new kinds of evidence, previously judged irrelevant, as the basis for reinterpreting history? Are we deluding ourselves in claiming that historians, unlike mythmakers, are unaffected by changing political concerns of the present in revising their views of the past?

The history of the PCI over the past decades shows how unclear the borders are between political myth and political history. Historians in fact occupied an important place in the ideological system of the Communist Party. Not only were scholars who focused on the history of the party—such as Paolo Spriano—involved in these efforts, but economic, social, political, and labor historians were involved, as well. Indeed, the PCI sponsored, directly or indirectly, many scholarly journals, research centers, and conferences devoted to the study of history. Their work—ranging from the history of the

Italian Unification to that of the early Socialist movement and agrarian protests, from the Resistance against Fascism to the rise of women's rights movements—provided a crucial component of party identity and ideology.

Most of this work was done by professional historians, who argued among themselves—as historians are supposed to—about sources, evidentiary bases for claims, and interpretations. Yet the problems selected for study changed according to political circumstances, and some topics and some interpretations were taboo. Many professional historians, for example, were employed at newly funded Institutes for the Study of the Resistance, devoted to the examination of a two-year period involving a limited part of the country, while virtually none were employed at Institutes for the Study of Fascism, although Fascist rule had lasted for two decades and involved the whole nation.[22]

The sacrality of the past is manufactured in many ways. Certain past episodes are constructed and made holy, endowed with a transcendent significance. In the case of the PCI, the sacred flames burned brightest for two events: the October Revolution—and with it the founding of the PCI itself—and the Resistance. Both became the subject of endless myth and ritual. Likewise, certain people were selected for deification, their lives endowed with a timeless meaning.

The Russian Revolution prompted tremendous enthusiasm among politicized workers throughout much of Western Europe. As for the PCI, the Revolution provided the party's rationale for being, its major source of identity in its early years. The Revolution linked the party to something much larger and more powerful than itself: the international Communist movement and, in particular, the new workers' state, the Soviet Union.

From the PCI's inception in 1921, party speeches, documents, and rituals were filled with references to 1917, the year of the Revolution. This year became the marker of the beginning of a new era, a sacred time of liminality. It was reified in such a way that one could be "on the side of the October Revolution," to use party head Luigi

Longo's proud phrase from 1969.[23] In PCI discourse, the Revolution was almost always referred to in terms of time rather than place: party leaders spoke glowingly not of the Russian Revolution but of the October Revolution. Time has the virtue of universality—it can be claimed by all—whereas the particularity of place carries certain disadvantages (not least of these being that it makes members subject to the suspicion of loyalty to another country).

At the celebration of the sixtieth anniversary of the October Revolution, held in Moscow in 1977, PCI head Enrico Berlinguer spoke of the Revolution in these terms:

> Dear Comrades,
>   I convey to you all the fraternal greetings of the P.C.I. With legitimate pride—as Comrade Brezhnev has said—the Communists and peoples of the Soviet Union are celebrating the sixtieth Anniversary of the victory of the October Socialist Revolution, sixty years of a tormented, difficult march, but rich with gains in planned economic development, in social justice and cultural elevation; and towering in this march is your decisive contribution to the victory over nazi-fascist barbarity, with the sacrifice of millions and millions of human lives, and your constant work to defend world peace.
>   With the Socialist Revolution of 1917, a radical change of course took place in history, and this is how the workers of all continents still see it today. The victory of Lenin's Party was of truly universal scope, because it broke the chain of domination by capitalism and imperialism, until then world-wide, and because for the first time it placed the principle of equality among all men at the foundation of the construction of a new society.

Berlinguer concluded his speech this way:

> All of us have a long road yet ahead of us. Nevertheless, we Italian Communists are certain that the Communist and Workers'

Parties, the liberation movements and the progressive forces in every country, developing the results of the October Revolution, according to the tasks and modes proper to each, will succeed—with the consequent universalization of democracy, freedom and the emancipation of labor—in overcoming the old capitalist system on a world scale and, thus, in securing a more serene, happy future for all the peoples.

We thank you, dear Comrades, for inviting us to these celebrations for the October Revolution, and we ask you to receive the warm best wishes that the Italian Communists convey to the workers and peoples of the Soviet Union for the success of the cause of peace and socialism.[24]

Berlinguer thus provides us with a classic example of the sacralization of history. The mythologized event has become heavily ritualized, to be celebrated each year. The ritual structure demands participation: were Berlinguer not to have taken part, were he to have sent a lower-ranking PCI officer to represent the party in the rites, a powerful message would have been sent, with serious political consequences. The ritualized salutation—Dear Comrades—is demanded by the grammar of the rite, expressing a solidarity and identity between the PCI and the rulers of the Soviet Union. Had a different salutation been used—Dear Friends, for example—its jarring note, immediately interpretable in terms of its contrast with the ritually required formula, would have signaled rupture.

In this process of sacralization, the PCI is personified, capable of "sending its greetings," and the leader of the USSR is identified as a comrade, one of "us." There then comes the direct construction of history, the panegyric to the Revolution, again referred to not as the Russian Revolution but as the October Socialist Revolution, reifying the complex web of activities, people, and events into a simple narrative structure.

The Revolution, in turn, is defined not in terms of what took place in 1917 but teleologically in terms of what took place in subsequent years. Berlinguer stresses the mythic themes of PCI history, especially the fight against "nazi-fascist barbarity" and against capitalism and imperialism. The Soviet Communist Party is identified as "Lenin's Party"; by contrast, identifying the CPSU in 1977 as Brezhnev's Party would have been not just inappropriate but baffling. Such a reference would also have been embarrassing, calling into question the putative democracy of the Soviet Communist Party in a way that reference to Lenin's Party did not.

The PCI sponsored events throughout Italy to commemorate the sixtieth anniversary of the October Revolution. At the most important of these, in connection with the national festa dell'Unità, party leader Paolo Bufalini spoke of the Revolution as an "event of decisive importance not only for contemporary history, but for the history of all mankind." The religious quality of his tribute comes through clearly in a torrent of party truisms crammed into a single sentence:

> Not only for us as Communists, but for everyone who nourishes the ideal of socialism and grasps the liberating value for all mankind of the October Revolution and everything that the presence of the Soviet Union . . . has meant and means in the struggle and victory over Nazism and fascism, in the fight for peace, disarmament and peaceful coexistence and cooperation among the peoples, in the struggle of the peoples for liberation from the colonial yoke . . . for everyone . . . who grasps these fundamental elements of contemporary history, but also for its enemies and adversaries, the October Revolution and what was born from it and built on it—a new society and a whole set of new societies in a large part of the world, indeed now in every continent—cannot but represent the outstanding event, the decisive innovation in contemporary history.[25]

In short, we have a kind of second coming, the dawning of a new era. Bufalini could hardly be clearer about what he was up to: the making of history.

In proposing a new future for the party, Occhetto would have to provide a new history. Here he faced a daunting task, for he was treading on sacred historical ground. History has to be remade carefully.

It should not be surprising, then, that in introducing the motion for the founding of the new party, Occhetto began by offering a new reading of the October Revolution. He built on the groundwork laid in the early 1980s by Enrico Berlinguer. The Revolution would remain a watershed of history, yet it would be stripped of its millennial qualities: "The historical process that gave rise to the worldwide Communist movement, the revolutionary turning point of October, and the societies that arose from that turning point, have entered a phase of organic crisis. . . . The failure of that model of social organization is irreversible." This statement came perilously close to a sacrilegious reading of the October Revolution, but Occhetto comforted the party faithful by adding, "The break of '17 opened the way to a glorious process of human emancipation, of consciousness raising, autonomously and independently entered into by the working classes and the popular masses. It opened the way for the liberation movement of countless peoples living in the colonial regimes. . . . The whole world was affected, and transformed, by this historical experience."[26] Occhetto thus sought to save the sacred symbolism of the October Revolution while distancing himself from it. He redefined the event so that its value was now to be found in the past rather than in the present.

Like the Soviet Communist Party, the PCI was personified through a series of mythic figures, its history inscribed in their lives. The lament of the prominent novelist Natalia Ginzburg, in her objection to the plan to change the party's name, was symptomatic: "For me," she wrote, "the Communist Party is the party of Gramsci, Togliatti, Terracini, and Berlinguer. . . . I can't think of the word *Communist* apart from them." She went on to contrast the false Communism of Stalin, Ceausescu, and Pol Pot with the "true Communism, which isn't repressive, which isn't bloody and isn't totalitarian—that found in the soul of Gramsci or Berlinguer." She concluded, "Are we who called ourselves Communist in the time of Stalin or Brezhnev supposed to stop calling ourselves Communist now that there is Gorbachev?"[27]

Throughout the debate on the svolta, party members, from leaders to simple activists, prefaced their recommendations with ritualized references to the wisdom of the party's leaders of the past. Typical of such prefatory obeisances were such openings as "today, when the richness of Gramsci's and Berlinguer's thoughts allows us to understand and make sense of the latest developments . . . "[28]

For the forces in favor of the svolta, the wand of legitimacy had to be waved, the blessings of the party deities invoked. In a typical invocation, Paolo Bufalini, after speaking in favor of the svolta, added, "This too is the classic strategy of the PCI, of Togliatti, of Longo, of Amendola." Meanwhile, the leaders of the opposition protested that the party must "preserve at least some of the characteristics that have made the old party of Gramsci, of Togliatti, and of Berlinguer so strong."[29]

The PCI leaders' self-consciousness about the importance of the past in defining the present is striking. As revered elder statesman Giancarlo Pajetta prefaced his remarks on the wisdom of the svolta, "I would first of all like to remind some comrades that even the present is made from the past, that there is the new because there is an old which took place, that Gramsci and Togliatti innovated what was left by Bordiga."[30]

Over time, new mythic figures arose—such as Enrico Berlinguer, whose death in the midst of an election campaign speech in the central Piazza of Padova in 1984 provided a suggestive setting for his apotheosis—and others were desanctified. No case of desanctification was more dramatic than that of Stalin, referred to characteristically in 1935 by party leader Togliatti as "Comrade Stalin, the leader, teacher, and friend of the proletariat and of all oppressed people."[31] Indeed, the treatment of Stalin offers the most dramatic example of the turning of party leaders into saints to be propitiated, in a form so clearly religious that it would later be totally erased from official party histories.

A good illustration of this is Togliatti's tribute to Stalin, published on the front page of the party's weekly journal in 1949. Had Stalin's name been replaced with "the Lord," Communism and Marxism-Leninism with "Christianity," and had other appropriate substitutions of idiom been made, the supplication would have fit smoothly into the Church's liturgy:

> In the name of the working class and of all those Italians in whose hearts lives a love of progress, for democracy and for peace, in the name of more than two million Italian communists, I most heartily send Comrade Stalin our best wishes, filled with devotion and affection.
>
> For many years our party has lived under the most difficult of conditions. We have succeeded in becoming a great party of the masses, thanks to the battle that the Communists have carried on, toppling the Fascist regime. But we would have hoped in vain, had it not been for You—leader, inspirer, clever chieftain.
>
> We know that without you, Comrade Stalin, the Italian people would find themselves today in much more difficult conditions. Thanks to you and your activities, in the decisive moments of this century the battle has been decided in favor of the working class, in favor of socialism.
>
> You have taught us how to be Communists, how to fight under any circumstances, how to be faithful to the very last principle of Marxism-Leninism and how to serve the cause of emancipation of the workers. We commit ourselves to be faithful to your teachings, to struggle for the unity of the workers, for the independence of our country, for peace; and against those who would provoke another war.
>
> We greatly admire and respect the invincible force of Marxism-Leninism in you, the invincible force of the working class, the highest realization of human ideals.

> We wish you a long life of good health, for the welfare of
> the people of the Soviet Union, for the welfare of the working
> class and the people of the entire world.
> Glory to you, Comrade Stalin.[32]

Long before the svolta, of course, Stalin's memory had been
desanctified and the party's formerly worshipful stance toward him
had become an embarrassment. It is notable, though, that the
desanctification of Stalin occurred not through any rejection of
the sacrality of party leaders. There was no critical eye turned on the
process by which party leaders became party saints; quite the contrary. The rejection of Stalin was legitimated by the invention of a
new narrative of party history focusing on a reinterpretation of the
history of Gramsci and Togliatti. Occhetto's comments in his opening address to the Twentieth Congress of the PCI in 1991 typified this
approach:

> Today, in ratifying the formation of the Democratic Party of the
> Left, I feel the need to say that this new initiative of the Left can-
> not but feel the influence of the highest moral force, the intel-
> lectual force of a philosophy that opposed all dogmatism, the
> thought of Gramsci. It was an outlook that indeed led him to be
> isolated in the context of international Communism, and that
> made him a thinker and political leader regarded as a heretic
> with respect to Stalinism. . . . Yes, for this reason too we will
> carry Gramsci with us, into the new party, we will carry him in
> our minds and in our hearts.[33]

The Political Construction of the Self Through History

We must all work continuously (if unselfconsciously) to construct
our sense of self, and in doing so we seek a sense of stability. No component of this process is more important than our efforts to provide
ourselves with a history. We seek, in these efforts, to tell a story about
ourselves, that is, to provide ourselves with a sense of continuity,
through which we relate ourselves to the larger world.

Any threat to the stability of our sense of the past threatens the stability of our sense of self. As David Lowenthal wrote in *The Past Is a Foreign Country*, "We need a stable past to validate tradition, to confirm our own identity, and to make sense of the present."[34] It is this sense of history that links us to larger entities—from ethnic group to nation to religion—and gives meaning and value to them.

For many of the members of the PCI, the sacred history of the party provided a key component of their sense of self. Any attempts to redefine history risked bringing their sense of self into question, a threat sure to provoke emotional reaction. For example, one party leader exclaimed, in reaction to Occhetto's initial proposal, "I am very worried. They mustn't abandon anything of what they are or what we were."[35]

The battle over the party's present and future, in becoming a battle over its history, inevitably became, too, a battle over the members' sense of self. Members felt threatened by the prospect of changing the kit of symbols by which they had constructed themselves. They reacted angrily by drawing on the sanctified symbols of party history to defend both their view of history and, ipso facto, their view of who they were.

Paolo Bufalini's initial reaction to Occhetto's announcement of the svolta is revealing: "However this project ends, even if I take part in such a new political group, I will continue to feel and to call myself a Communist, which I have been from '37 to today, and which—pardon me for saying so—I declared in front of the special [Fascist] tribunal in 1942."[36] Bufalini's sense of self in the present was thus based on a sense of history that linked him to a sacred past: the struggle against Fascism and events that took place more than a half century before.

Innumerable letters to the party newspaper from distraught members show a similar disillusionment. In an angry letter to Occhetto, an elderly woman, an agricultural wage laborer from the Bologna area, protested the changing of the party name: "Under the Fascist terror, enduring persecution, beatings, jail, the destruction of my house and the killing of my mother, I . . . became a rebel. And I was called a Communist and a Bolshevik by the Fascists: it was an honor."[37]

In the battle over the proposed svolta, Occhetto and his allies were more vulnerable to attacks of disparaging the past than they were to the much less emotional charge that they were disrupting the present. The accusation of "repudiating our past" became the opposition's cri de coeur.[38]

Occhetto, in defense, felt obliged to deny that his proposal implied a rejection of the past; indeed, he could not even admit that he was promoting a redefinition of the past. Yet his claim of embracing (even celebrating) the past had, necessarily, to be based on a ceaseless effort to redefine it. A new future required a new past. This new past consisted of a party whose history was one of total independence from the USSR, a past in which the party not only had refrained from supporting the totalitarian regimes of the Communist countries but had been instrumental in overthrowing them.

The Narrative Structure of History

If the past is sacred and provides the self with a sense of continuity and structure, then it follows that the past itself comes to have a certain kind of structure, infused with sacrality. In the PCI version of history, the symbolism of Fascism and anti-Fascism, capitalism and Communism, bosses and workers, imperialists and freedom-fighters offered a basic structure. On one side evil, on the other good; on one side the rich and powerful, on the other the (morally deserving) oppressed and the poor. History in this schema consisted of a battle, a war between good and evil; this history thus lent itself to religious and military metaphors.[39]

The bellicose and religious interpretation of history permits the collapsing of all time; history is lived. Yesterday's battles are today's battles, yesterday's demons today's. Occhetto's most implacable foes within the party, for example, felt it necessary to preface their dissenting motion, presented to the Nineteenth Party Congress in 1990, with a historical rationale: "In this situation," they explained in the preamble, "our country needs combatants for an effective democracy more than ever, and democracy, too, needs the Communists, a strong and great Communist party, more than ever." The historical basis for this claim then follows: "In fact, the Italian Communists have been the decisive unitary force in the anti-Fascist battle that led to the Republican Constitution, in the struggle to safeguard that Constitution in 1960, when workers, partigiani and young people led by the PCI overcame the danger of neo-Fascist restoration, in the social struggles of 1968–75 in which masses of men and women, once more led by the working-class and its party . . . "[40]

Here the Communists are portrayed as combatants for democracy, needed now more than ever because of what they had done in the past. In this mix of the past and present, the Resistance has no end, as is indicated by the reference to the battle against Fascist restoration in 1960, involving the "partisans" one more time. No one would think of referring to someone who had been a high school student in 1945 as a "student" in 1960, yet once one becomes a partisan, one is a partisan all one's life. One identity (partisan), constructed of history, is mythic; the other (student) is not.

Among the most powerful narrative structures used by party leaders and members were those that combined military and religious imagery by focusing on the symbolism of sacrifice and, in particular, on the ultimate sacrifice, death. In the immediate aftermath of Occhetto's proposal, for example, a party member from Asti, his anger unmistakable, begged the party paper to publish his letter so that Occhetto would read it and take notice:

There are comrades who used blood from their own veins to write "Viva Communism" on the walls of their Fascist jail cells; comrades who rather than ask Mussolini for a pardon (which

would have meant renouncing their entire political faith) spent
years and years in prison. Comrades who standing before the
execution squad shouted "Viva Italy! Viva Communism!"
        This is what I wanted to say to Occhetto . . . I and so many
others like me are not ashamed to call ourselves Communists.[41]

Again, the present is justified in terms of the past, a sacralized past
referring to events of more than half a century before. The Christo-
logical nature—or, more generally, the martyrology—of the symbolism is hard to miss: the Communists were like the early Christians
under the Romans, or the Jews under the Spanish Inquisition, all
refusing to renounce their "faith."
        Another member, a retired sixty-eight-year-old working-class
woman, tells of joining the party in 1947. Her plea against Occhetto's
proposal is similarly based on historical argument. Hers is an interpretation of history that leads to a particular interpretation of the
present, because it offers a particular definition of the self. She
explains, "I have always battled alongside all the workers to change
things in our country, which was left in ruins by the war and then
governed by the conservative forces." Her tale of sacrifice and martyrdom continues, "I was, like so many other brave and courageous
comrades—both men and women—persecuted, fired from my job,
put on trial and twice sent to jail. And so many have died with the
name of the PCI on their lips."[42] She thus begins her letter by asserting a claim to moral authority that comes from having joined the
party during the legendary time of the immediate postwar period.
She employs military symbolism to describe both the actual fighting
of the war and subsequent labor disputes. When she recalls the striking workers who were killed by police in the period of DC-backed
violent repression of labor unrest from the 1950s through 1960, and
describes them as dying "with the name of the PCI on their lips," the
various periods of history and spheres of political activity become
intermingled in a powerful image that gives meaning not just to history but also, clearly, to the woman's sense of self.[43]

A remarkably similar statement reveals the pervasiveness of this symbolism. An older comrade, in a letter to Occhetto, denounced him for having "repudiated seventy years of Communist history!" What, the man asked, would Occhetto respond "to all those who were sent into exile, persecuted, who fought in Spain [in the Spanish Civil War], to all the partigiani who died with 'io sono comunista' [I am Communist] on their lips and who live eternally in our hearts as martyrs of the PCI?"[44] Likewise, in another letter to Occhetto, a woman from Parma lamented the imminent loss of the party name and symbols: "For those of us of a certain age it was always our symbol, we waged so many struggles, we lost so many comrades in the streets, and now I ask myself: for what did they die?"[45]

These military and religious themes were not conceived of individually by party members; rather, they reflect a narrative structure promulgated by the party organization. The PCI statutes, which were widely distributed to the members, offer one such source for this officially authorized historical narrative structure. These statutes spelled out the party's ideology in a way suitable for use in socializing members. It is significant that the first part of the statutes does not concern rules of the party at all but, instead, offers an official account of the party's history. This preamble to the statutes (I use the text approved in 1975) develops the principal myths on which the historical identity of the party rested:

> The Italian Communist Party is the political organization of the vanguard of the working class and of all the workers who, in the spirit of the Resistance and of proletarian internationalism and in the practice of class struggle, fight to ensure the country's independence and liberty, to build a democratic and progressive government, to eliminate the exploitation of one man by another, for liberty and the full expression of the human personality, for peace among all peoples, and for socialism.
>
> The Italian Communist Party was formed in 1921, at the Congress of Livorno, on the basis of the experience of the Ital-

ian workers' movement, and the teachings of Marx and Lenin and the momentum given to the international workers' movement by the October Revolution. It brought together in its ranks the most advanced portion, and the best traditions, of the Italian Socialist Party. With its formation, the Italian Communist Party gave the workers, the intellectuals, and the masses of the exploited an ideological, political, and organizational guide in the struggle for liberty and socialism. The Italian Communist Party, inspired by the teachings of Antonio Gramsci and Palmiro Togliatti, courageously resisted the Fascist criminal tyranny, combating it in every way within the country and on the battlefields. . . . it promoted national anti-Fascist solidarity against Fascism and the Nazi invader, it participated in a decisive way in the direction and the victory of the War of Liberation.

With the country liberated and the Fascist regime liquidated, the Italian Communist Party was and remains at the head of the popular masses in reforming the political, economic, and social institutions of Italy. It battled to ensure that the new republican constitution would be inspired by the principles of the Resistance.[46]

The reliance of the party on the symbolism of the Resistenza could hardly be more evident. Note, too, the way in which the military metaphor of the Resistance is carried over to other "struggles." In mythic time historically disparate events become intermingled, as seen in the preamble's first paragraph, in which the postwar politics of the PCI are equated with the struggle during the Resistance for national independence and the establishment of democracy. The religious quality also comes across in this first paragraph, with its millenarian goals of ending all evil and allowing the full "expression of the human personality."

The second paragraph paints a portrait of the sacred past, linked to the party's identification with the fight against Fascism. It invokes two of the party's saints—Marx and Lenin—as part of its origin myth, defining the Bolshevik-inspired walkout from the Socialist Party in 1921 as a matter of the emergence of the "most advanced" part of the Socialist Party. Two other party saints—Gramsci and Togliatti—are recalled to characterize and legitimate the subsequent years of party life under Fascism, and the party is given primary responsibility for the defeat of the Nazis. Even following Liberation, in this account, the party continued its battle, now applying the military metaphor of the Resistance, fighting to "ensure that the new republican constitution would be inspired by the principles of the Resistance."

In the struggle over becoming post-Communist, interpretations of history thus came to play a major role. We can now look directly at the strategies of each side in the pci struggle of 1989–91.

chapter six

Alternative Histories

Opposition to the Svolta

The relation of the PCI's history to recent events in Eastern Europe and the Soviet Union (and, to a lesser extent, China) was the main battleground of the fight over the party's future. Whether or not the PCI, as a "Communist" party, was somehow compromised by these events became a matter of interpreting history. The view that the PCI should become post-Communist as a result of these developments represented, in the view of the opposition, an admission that the PCI was rightfully identified with the Communist parties and regimes of the Communist countries. This identification was one that even the party leadership could not directly admit. Opposition leaders not only rejected this construction of the party's history, they worked mightily to craft an alternative history, employing the sacrality of the PCI's history to discredit the party leaders who called for change.

In this view of history, Communism was divided, at least since Lenin's time, between good Communism and bad Communism. The bad Communism was the Communism of Stalin and his successors in both the USSR and the rest of the Communist world. The good Communism was that of the PCI, which had always opposed the bad Communism. In this vein, Giuseppe Chiarante, one of the more prominent opponents of the svolta, argued that the PCI was entitled to assert its blamelessness from the sins of the bad Communism "because it had at its roots such thought as that of Gramsci, which was radically anti-Stalinist." He went on to add, "Togliatti had already created the 'new party.'"[1]

Given the power of Resistance symbolism within the party, it is not surprising that many of the attempts to discredit Occhetto's plan

108

used the equation of the PCI with the Resistance as an argument for leaving the PCI intact. Any questioning of the PCI's existing symbolism thus meant questioning the validity of the myth of the Resistance. The comments of a Communist auto worker, born more than two decades after the war's end, typify the kind of reification prevalent among party members: "Why change the name? That glorious name and symbol were behind the anti-Fascist movement and the Resistance."[2]

More generally, any way in which the Resistance could be recalled and linked to the PCI became a means for legitimating the opposition. Consider the logic employed by Giancarlo Pajetta, the party leader whose negative comments immediately following Occhetto's announcement of the svolta presaged the battle that lay ahead. In announcing his opposition to the proposal, Pajetta lost no time in linking the question of future decisions to the interpretation of the past, stating, "I am not ashamed of this name nor of our history." He continued, "When Longo sent me to Parri to organize the command of the [Committees of National Liberation], neither Parri nor anyone else asked me to change the name but only asked that we fight together."[3] Pajetta thus identified himself with Luigi Longo, revered in PCI history as one of the principal leaders of the Resistance, later to become party head. Ferruccio Parri, another of the Resistance leaders but not a Communist, is the other principal player in this historical narrative that has a double track: a gloss for past events and a model for interpreting the present.[4]

This political construction of history was not merely the preserve of the old, nor was it limited to those who could claim direct contact with the heroic events of the mythic past. Consider the following letter to L'Unità from a Communist youth (FGCI) section, giving the members' reasons for opposing the svolta:

A hammer and a sickle bring to mind sensations, experiences, emotions, martyrs from the world of work and martyrs for liberty, positions of conscience, alternative values and cultures, but above all they bring to mind justice and liberty at all times of our history. A name and a symbol that are rooted in the Resistance and anti-Fascism, in the postwar peasant struggles, in the unending advances of the working class, in Togliatti's new party . . . inspired by the only socialist state then victorious, and holding closely to the principles of Marxism-Leninism, even while indicating our own original Italian path to socialism.

. . . Marxism-Leninism produced very clearly a model of society that, through various stages, was to be constructed. Marx and Lenin bear no responsibility if some of those speaking in their name who appeared on the political scene somehow undermined their objectives.[5]

Here the party's symbols are directly equated with and defined by the party's history. This history is rooted in the mythic figures of Marx and Lenin, who are beyond criticism. Those who soiled this history—who go nameless—had nothing to do with the PCI, which, instead, is identified with the Resistance and the party's saints: Togliatti and Berlinguer.

The opposition's use of history did not go unchallenged by the forces in favor of the svolta, although party leaders did not dare to puncture the party's myths directly. By contrast, Mario Pirani, an old leader of the Left who was not a party member, did just this in an opinion piece appearing in *L'Unità* in March 1990. In disputing the way that the opposition was making history, Pirani had the freedom to call into question the sacred PCI past in a way Occhetto could not. He charged the opposition leaders with hypocrisy. They were guilty, he wrote, of twisting historical memory, inventing a PCI that had nothing to do with Stalinism. In this warped account, he argued, the PCI had somehow been "purified by its specific peculiarity" and thus was incapable of committing "misdeeds comparable to those perpetrated by parties that past congresses called 'brothers.'" They somehow forget, he continued, that the PCI heartily subscribed to the policies of the Comintern and the Cominform, which "led to the marginalization of Gramsci, to the expulsion of Spinelli and Terracini, to the condemnation of Silone, to the vilification of Tito, to the Moscow trials, to the gallows of Prague, and the tanks of Budapest." All this, he concluded, "seems completely forgotten or, indeed, as though it had never existed."[6] This was dangerous stuff, and neither Occhetto nor his principal allies in the party could take such a direct tack.

Arguing for the Svolta: Remaking Present and Past

Occhetto's approach to reinventing the past was much more subtle. Indeed, given the aggressive use made of the past by the opposition, Occhetto felt constrained to preface virtually all his remarks with a bow toward the PCI's glorious and unsullied history.

In formally presenting the new party name and symbol, for example, Occhetto assured his audience that in the first article of the new party statutes, "reference to the historical function and founding role of the Italian Communists in the new party will be made clear and explicit." This historical function, Occhetto went on to say, "cannot be erased, nor can it be hidden, because, unlike what happened in the other parties of Eastern Europe, we have behind us a past of which—despite the errors that we ourselves have denounced—we are proud."[7]

This is a rather curious passage. It suggests that the recognition of the Italian Communists' historical function and founding role in creating the PDS depended on the fact that, unlike other Communist parties, the PCI had an untainted past. We see in these remarks, too, the effort to distinguish the good Communism of the PCI from the bad Communism of the others. While "errori"—diplomatically not specified—had been committed, these had all been long since recognized and repudiated.

Occhetto enlisted the aid of history from the beginning of his quest. He had, after all, chosen the ceremonies commemorating the anniversary of a Resistance battle as the occasion for announcing the svolta. Through his speech there he sought to link his own plans for change to the sacred Resistance symbolism. Thus he counterposed the need to ensure, through such commemorative rites, that the "values of the national liberation struggle would be transmitted to the new generations" with the apparently unrelated observation that "the construction of this [Berlin] Wall was not in the spirit of the Resistance."[8]

Occhetto subsequently sought to legitimate the svolta by drawing comparisons to hallowed events in the history of the PCI, in effect trying to reenact the sacred past in the heretical present.[9] Given the consternation that greeted his remarks at Bolognina, Occhetto was asked whether his proposal might not lead some members to leave the party. He replied by saying that most party members understood that to remain unchanged "would be an act contrary to the best of our tradition." It would be, he continued, "as if in '44, instead of choosing the path of national unity and a Constituent Assembly, we had followed the path of the parties that accepted the logic of Leninist Bolshevization." "To remain unchanged today," Occhetto concluded, "would be as if Berlinguer had not made the break [with the Soviet bloc] in the face of the events in Poland."[10]

In his political struggle Occhetto made use not only of the symbolic content of the PCI history but, at a deeper level, of the Communist theory of history, what Karl Popper, in *The Poverty of Historicism*, disparagingly referred to as Marxist historicism. Recall, for example, Occhetto's comments on the "historical function" of the Italian Communists. The PCI had served its historical function; now history called on the Communists to move to the next historical stage. In keeping with this view of the march of history, Occhetto, at the first national party festival following the formation of the PDS, announced that the fall of the Berlin Wall was ushering in the "beginning of a new history."[11] It was a new history that evidently required a new party.

The Resistance

No historical symbol carried more weight in the PCI than the Resistenza, and a complex web of symbolism and ritual was erected around it. Hundreds of party sections were named after martyred partisans, shrines to partisans—adorned with their pictures and regularly propitiated with flowers—dotted the streets of the center and north of the country, the PCI regularly sponsored commemorations of all sorts, and the legitimacy of a whole generation of party leaders was assured by their own personal claims to having been partigiani.

In the form advanced by the PCI over the previous forty-five years, the history of the Resistance can be simply told: led by the Communists, the Italian people rose up against Fascism and their Nazi occupiers in 1943, fighting a heroic battle against superior forces for two years, until, as a result of their efforts, the Nazi-Fascists were defeated. The Resistance was made strong by the willingness of all anti-Fascist forces to work together, but the bulk of the combatants and most of those martyred in the struggle were Communists.

How closely this account corresponds to an outside historian's interpretation of the evidence is not our main concern. Most non-Communist histories, though, tell a different story, one in which the defeat of the Nazis was primarily the result of the Allied military forces, and in which the mushrooming of the Resistance forces corresponded only in part to the spread of Communist or patriotic ideals. In the face of conscription by the Nazi-Fascist forces, many young men were left the alternative of being shipped off to the Russian front or taking to the hills and joining the Resistance.[12]

The history of the Resistance provided by the PCI proved to have great appeal in postwar Italy. Mussolini's long reign was a national embarrassment, and people sought a history that was heroic rather than cowardly. In this new construction of history, Italians were to be seen not as co-conspirators who were partially responsible for the horrors of the Second World War but as victims who heroically rose up to slay the evil that had been thrust upon them.

From the perspective of the PCI, this Resistance-focused history not only had the virtue of assigning the party a heroic role but, perhaps as important, established its patriotic credentials. Indeed, in the years following the war no symbol of nationalism was more powerful than the Resistance, and no patriotic credential was more valuable than having been a partisan. For a party that—partially as a result of its banishment and persecution in Fascist Italy—had long been a creature of the USSR, a party whose head was long based in Moscow and not in Rome, this kind of symbolic transformation proved invaluable.

The appeal of this history of the Resistance was so great that the PCI's competitors dealt gingerly with it (with the notable exception of the neo-Fascist MSI). The Christian Democrats, too, sought to identify themselves with the Resistance, although there were clearly mixed feelings in the DC about this, especially from some of the more conservative clerical forces. The Christian Democrats competed by naming some of their sections after fallen "partisans" of their own, and the DC did what it could to prevent the symbolism and rites surrounding the Resistance from becoming completely monopolized by the PCI.[13]

An instructive parallel is to be found in France. As Henry Rousso put it, the French were able to "repress memories of the civil war with the aid of what came to be a dominant myth: '*resistancialism*.'" The myth consisted, on one hand, of minimizing the significance (indeed, insofar as possible, erasing the memory) of the Vichy regime and the extent of popular complicity in it. On the other, it involved the "construction of an object of memory, the 'Resistance,' whose significance transcended by far the sum of its active parts (the small groups of guerrilla partisans who did the actual fighting)." Although the Gaullists and the Communists invoked quite different versions of this myth, they shared an interest in its primary elements: "exaggerating the scope of French resistance" and "minimizing the role of Vichy."[14]

For both the French and the Italians, the time of the Resistance was sacred. It was a liminal period when the normal social structure had broken down and people escaped their previous lives and roles, giving them the possibility of defining new selves. It was in this fertile soil that the Italian Communist Party could offer people a new identity by means of a new history.

The liminality, and even romanticism, of the period is reflected in one of the more curious practices found among the groups of armed men who hid in the hills and mountains of northern Italy in the winter of 1944. Many partigiani gave up their old names—presumably to provide greater security through anonymity—and assumed names that identified them with their rural environment, such as Volpe (Fox), Lupo (Wolf), Corvo (Crow), and Pecora (Sheep), or Terremoto (Earthquake), Fulmine (Lightning), Saetta (Thunderbolt), Tempesta (Storm), and Turbine (Whirlwind).[15] These names became the source of a new and sacred identity. In later years, the most emotionally powerful way to link a person to the Resistance was to call him by his nom de guerre.

Given the centrality of this Resistance symbolism to the party, it is hardly surprising that the history of the Resistance loomed so large in the polemics over the party's future that erupted practically a half century after the war's end. The sacred time of the Resistance and the profane time of the present were to become mixed, following a logic characteristic of mythic thought.

Occhetto employed a wide variety of symbolic means to associate himself and the new direction of the party with the Resistance. At the same time, his opponents did all they could to identify him with the desecration of its memory.

When he first presented the svolta to the party Central Committee, Occhetto varied the Resistance theme, railing against "totalitarian states that have usurped the name of socialism, obscuring the great political and moral potential of the Resistance and of the victorious struggle against Nazi-Fascism."[16] With rather peculiar logic, he thus vilified the USSR and the East European regimes for having defiled the sacred memory of the Resistance.

These attempts to identify the new course with the Resistance did not go unchallenged. The emotion that this use of Resistance history generated is nicely illustrated in a column written in the Bologna pages of *L'Unità* in early 1990. Gino Milli, the head of a local chapter of the Associazione nazionale dei partigiani italiani (ANPI), the partisan veterans' association, wrote:

> Comrade Occhetto and his supporters cannot profit from the fact that his proposal was launched on the occasion of a demonstration he attended, a demonstration in which the glorious victims of the partisan battle of Bolognina were commemorated. And his action gives the mistaken impression that the partisans support his proposal. All the more so because . . . there is a great contradiction between what Occhetto proposed and the reason for which the partisans of that battle died so heroically. . . .
>
> Comrade Occhetto, while posing the problem of radically changing our way of doing politics and our very way of being, claims that the moment is right for a decisive turnabout, even at the cost of throwing in the garbage can both the name and the emblem of the party and, indeed, throwing out our very identity, which includes the sacrifice of our heroes and of thousands of partisans who have battled for this identity for over forty-five years.
>
> The partisans, indeed, believe that this is a shameful manner of abdicating the decisive role that awaits the Italian Communist Party.[17]

Here the battle over history is joined, and the link between the representation of that history and current struggles for power is made clear. Milli first connects the dead heroes of the Resistance with the PCI and then imputes to them a motive for which they fought against the Nazis, namely, the defense of the Communist party. The collapsing of history follows, as the "sacrifice" of these partisans is extended to include their battles for more than forty-five years, all devoted to the Communist cause. The Resistance lives. Although he castigates Occhetto for attempting to "strumentalizzare" (exploit) the history of the Resistance, Milli does exactly the same thing, presenting himself as representative for all partigiani.

The Triangle of Death

The fragile nature of the past, and the complexities of doing political battle through history, are well illustrated by a series of events that unfolded in September 1990. The catalyst, ironically, came from an elderly local PCI office-holder in Reggio Emilia, a former partisan, Otello Montanari, who had organized a conference on unresolved questions regarding events in the immediate postwar period. At issue was the history of the Triangolo della Morte (triangle of death) circumscribed by Bologna, Modena, and Reggio Emilia. In this heavily Communist area, partisans had been slow to disarm following the war's end and, according to some reports, had slaughtered hundreds if not thousands of unarmed men they deemed Fascists. The question was not simply whether such events occurred—and whether they could be symbolically linked to the Resistance—but what their relation was to the PCI. In particular, the party head, Palmiro Togliatti, who was minister of justice in the coalition government at the time, was charged with protecting the perpetrators, shielding them from justice in part by arranging for hundreds to flee Italy and take refuge in Communist countries.

At stake here, too, was the historical image the PCI presented of itself as having been dedicated above all in these immediate postwar years to establishing parliamentary democracy in Italy. As Massimo D'Alema, second only to Occhetto in the party hierarchy, put it, "The historical judgment regarding the party of those years is precise: the PCI disarmed the masses at the end of the Resistance and led them back to democracy."[18] The party's critics long sought to discredit this version of history, accusing party leaders of having practiced duplicity by publicly espousing a commitment to parliamentary democracy while many party members harbored—and, in the case of the Triangolo della Morte, acted on—the longtime Communist ideal of revolution and proletarian, one-party rule.[19]

As the conference approached, articles on the contested history of the Triangolo della Morte began appearing in the national press, and representatives of various political parties began to warm to the theme. The right-wing Italian Social Movement (MSI), defined by its own relation to the Fascist past, saw an opportunity for profitable symbolic activity and organized a demonstration to denounce deeds associated with the Triangle of Death. The MSI demonstration was scheduled to be held in the center of Reggio Emilia, a city long ruled by the PCI, posing a direct symbolic challenge to the PCI's sacred space.[20]

All this came about at a time when the PCI was riven by factionalism, seemingly paralyzed by the ferocity of the battle between Occhetto's forces and those opposing him. With its sacred history challenged from without, though, leaders on both sides faced a complicated symbolic calculus. External threats to the party's sacred symbolism could normally be counted on to produce solidarity in the party, the immediate pulling together of all "comrades" in emotional counterattack. Moreover, the historical account being challenged was one employed by both party factions. The extent to which each faction defended the PCI version of postwar history itself became an element in the factional dispute. In this battle, the proponents of the svolta found themselves under greatest pressure, for they were already under attack by the opposition for abandoning the party's patrimonio, for liquidating its history.

These cross-cutting currents led initially to expressions of party solidarity uniting both factions, based on the spinning of a singular historical narrative concerning the Resistance and the party in the immediate postwar years. The first reports of party reactions to the

Triangle of Death attacks stressed just this apparent effect: attacked (through history) by outsiders, divided party members showed a united front. A story published in *La Repubblica* on September 6, datelined Reggio Emilia, is typical: "Now enough, hands off the Resistance. . . . the PCI raises its voice. And reclaiming the pride of the party in the midst of the war between the 'yes' and the 'no' forces, they march in single battle formation against the 'political aggression' aimed at its entire past—both remote and recent." The party had decided, the newspaper went on to recount, to hold a national demonstration in Reggio Emilia the following Sunday "in defense of the Liberation struggle."[21]

The temptation to use this powerful history for factional benefit, though, was irresistible. The precipitating event was a newspaper interview with Piero Fassino, a close collaborator of Occhetto, who acted as the party's official speaker on the controversy. The interviewer asked him whether there was any truth to the charge that then Minister of Justice Palmiro Togliatti knew about plans for the escape abroad of people involved in "certain episodes." Shockingly—for party members—Fassino responded by admitting this, adding, "That choice does not seem justified to me. Togliatti placed the welfare of the party first, subordinating all others to it. This was the error, and we must still today come to terms with it."

The reaction from the opposing faction was swift, a ringing denunciation of the sacrilege not only for tarnishing the memory of the Resistance but for calling into question the saintly status of Togliatti. Indeed, with party members already inflamed by their leaders' denunciations of the "cowardly" assaults on the Resistance, the oppositionists in the party saw their opportunity. "I surmise from Fassino's remarks," proclaimed one PCI senator on the side of the opposition, "that the episode that has exploded in Reggio Emilia has been, at least in part and nefariously, hatched from within the party." Opposition leaders angrily called for Fassino's resignation.[22]

Occhetto's forces were placed in an awkward position, for the events appeared to offer a good opportunity for them to craft a new reading of the history of the Resistance. The Triangle of Death incident could be used to help redefine the party past in such a way as to justify the need for a change in the present. Further, offering such a new reading of history could itself help show skeptical outsiders that the party was not simply engaged in a change of window dressing but was mounting a major, substantive transformation. This is what likely lay behind Fassino's remarks.

Yet this approach to history was hazardous, and Occhetto himself was careful to keep his distance. Considerable benefit could be gained by taking quite a different approach. By doing everything they could to publicize and magnify the incident—while decrying the fact that enemies of the party were keeping the issue alive—the PCI leaders could portray the episode as an attack on the Resistance and on the party itself. In this way, they could hope to reinvigorate the emotional links binding members and sympathizers to the party. This was a particularly attractive tactic because Occhetto's main concern at this time was the potential for a schism, the possibility that leaders of the opposition might succeed in luring large numbers of members to a breakaway party. Anything that could be done to increase party solidarity was to be seized upon.

That Occhetto was at least partially successful can be illustrated by an emotional letter to *L'Unità* penned in December 1990. The author, a Sicilian party activist, begins by admitting that he had voted for the opposition motion in his section congress earlier that year. He had done this, he explained, "because I essentially believe that we have nothing to be ashamed of in our tradition and in our struggles." Yet, he wrote, as a result of recent events he had changed his mind and now sided with Occhetto, "because I think it's absurd to continue to speak of motions or splits at a time in which everyone is attacking us, even questioning the Liberation struggle."[23]

In short, Occhetto chose not to follow the path on which Fassino disastrously set out. Instead, he employed the Triangle of Death incident to promote an emotional rallying around the party flag in the face of outside threats to the history of the Resistance.

Nowhere was this tactic clearer than in his address to the national party festival at the end of September 1990. Occhetto's address came shortly after the death of longtime party luminary Giancarlo Pajetta, who, like so many party leaders of that generation, derived great political benefit from his association with the Resistance:

> You have all seen, and we have all heard, countless confused words, insinuations, insults, and lies directed in these weeks against the PCI and against the Resistance. And, right at the height of this despicable campaign, our dear Gian Carlo Pajetta, partisan Nullo [Pajetta's nom de guerre], one of the clearest symbols of the Resistance, died. With his death, Pajetta caused the truth to reemerge; the story of his life and of his sacrifices has forced everyone to remember that nothing can call into question the Liberation struggle. It just takes the memory of a life like his to tell it all about the real values embodied in the Resistance. So we must react firmly to a campaign aimed at besmirching that which was, in the concrete life of countless courageous men, the real experience of the anti-Fascist Resistance militia. For nothing good can be done for the future by destroying the good that was done in the past.[24]

In considering first the power of the name and then, in these past two chapters, the power of history, I have been investigating the nature of symbolic capital. The symbolic capital in question is of a particular kind, involving the representations that political leaders provide to their followings. The representations offer both a reified notion of the group—in this case, the political party—and a satisfying sense of self.

These representations are promulgated in a variety of ways, not least of which these days are modern means of media, television foremost among them. But the most powerful mechanism for spreading them, for combining a particular view of the world with a particu-

larly powerful emotional attitude, is ritual. In the struggle to transform a Communist party to one that would be post-Communist, ritual provided a means for the party leadership to forge a new identity
for the party and its members. Yet ritual forms offered a potent
weapon for the opposition as well.

chapter seven

The Ritual Struggle

The Italian Communist Party could hardly be accused of ignoring the political value of ritual. Rites appeared at all levels of party activity and organization, from the daily rites of local party sections to the vast national rites embodied in annual party feste and periodic party congresses.

In examining PCI ritual and the use of ritual in the battle over the transformation of the party, I adopt a concept of ritual that is not limited to religion. Following many other analysts of ritual, and especially those concerned with its political uses, I take a broader view, identifying as ritual any symbolic behavior that is socially standardized, repetitive, and meaningful. Indeed, it is through ritual that symbols come to be defined, diffused, and energized.[1]

At the heart of the struggle over the transformation of the PCI was a battle over symbols, and the battle was fought in good part through ritual. Ritual forms proved of special value because it is through ritual that political myths can be most effectively promulgated.

Likewise, it is through the crucible of ritual that people link themselves and are seen by others to be linked to larger, symbolically constructed entities. The sense of self constructed by the individual Communist was based in part on a sense of continuity provided by participation in familiar rites. By regularly engaging in the same party-identified rituals, the members were provided reassurance that both their world and their selves had not changed, despite all the threats around them. As Barbara Myerhoff put it, "Ritual connects past, present, and future, abrogating history and time."[2] I shall return later to the apparent paradox of ritual as both abrogating history and serving as a key means for its construction.

Although ritual played a crucial part in the PCI-PDS transformation, its significance was largely denied—at least in public—by the principal contenders for power in the party. In the Marxist intellectual culture from which the PCI leaders came, ritual had a bad name. Political decisions were supposed to be based on "objective" circumstances and "scientific" reasoning. Ritual, by contrast, was identified with religion and superstition, in short, with the irrational.[3]

Recognition that ritual plays an important role in fostering political change does, however, have an important pedigree in Italian Marxist thought, traceable to Antonio Gramsci. Gramsci recognized that the success of a political movement was based less on its leaders' ability to convert people through debate than on its ability to use social and symbolic means of suasion:

> The popular element 'feels' but does not always know or understand; the intellectual element 'knows' but does not always understand and in particular does not always feel. . . . The intellectual's error consists in believing that one can know without understanding and even more without feeling and being impassioned . . . in other words that the intellectual can be an intellectual (and not a pure pedant) if distinct and separate from the people-nation, that is, without feeling the elementary passions of the people, understanding them and therefore explaining and justifying them in the particular historical situation. . . . One cannot make politics-history without this passion, without this sentimental connection between intellectuals and people-nation. In the absence of such a nexus the relations between the intellectual and the people-nation are, or are reduced to, relationships of a purely bureaucratic and formal order; the intellectuals become a caste, or a priesthood.[4]

Building on Gramsci's views, I view ritual as a central means by which political leaders are able to tap the passions of their groups' members and sympathizers. But ritual does more than simply stir the emotions.

The Power of Ritual

What is it about ritual that makes it so valuable to political leaders? Anthropologists, sociologists, and historians have long recognized the political uses of ritual, and I draw on their accumulated wisdom. But this literature has a significant limitation: it tends to equate political ritual with the reinforcement of the status quo. The value of ritual, though, goes well beyond shoring up existing power holders and power systems by surrounding them with legitimacy. Ritual is no less crucial to movements of political change than to champions of conservation. In this theoretical context, the case of the transformation of the PCI is especially enlightening, for, paradoxically, it pits a dominant power-holding group advocating change with a minority that seeks to prevent it.

To understand the role played by ritual in this situation, I distinguish four aspects of the political value of ritual: (1) its value in providing symbolic representation of the party; (2) its value in legitimation and mystification; (3) its value in promoting solidarity among party members; and (4) its value in fostering particular understandings of political reality.[5]

Representing the Party

Political parties can exist only through symbolic representation. Rites are crucial in the process by which individuals are identified with these symbolic entities. Through the party-associated rites, individuals both identify themselves with the party and become identified with it by others. Rituals allow individuals to come in contact with the holy symbols that bond them to this symbolic entity. Rituals provide a context in which the myths that sustain the party can be validated and kept alive. They also perform a crucial organizational function in distinguishing the "in" group from the "out" group, by making public the link between member or sympathizer and party symbol. Through the rites, the people proclaim their symbolic descent from common ancestors whose mythic status is promulgated through the rites themselves.[6]

Ritual not only provides individuals with group identities; it also magnifies perceived differences between one's own group and others by creating a symbolic universe in which groups can be conceived, made palpable, and assigned moral qualities. The ineffable is made natural.[7]

For the leaders of the PCI, the centrality of ritual in defining the party and in linking large numbers of people to it had profound implications. For the new "thing" to be considered *new* required new symbolic representation, yet at the same time the rites that linked members and sympathizers to the party were threatened by any rejection of the earlier symbolism on which the rites were based. Party rites without red flags, without the singing of various old revolutionary songs, without the old symbolic representation of the Communist heroes and the imperialist villains, would not be party rites at all.

The tendency of rites to clearly mark off one political group from another, that is, to provide tangible boundaries, became a potential pitfall for the proponents of the svolta. Occhetto and his allies were calling for the creation of a "new political formation," not a party, and they believed that the imminent demise of the Cold War afforded new possibilities for creating a broader alliance. The new entity, they argued, would be not simply a continuation of the old PCI under a new name but, rather, a coming together of people from a wide variety of groups previously outside the party: environmentalists, feminists, civil libertarians, and others. Indeed, scattered throughout the country, various clubs were founded by non–PCI members sympathetic to Occhetto's proposal. These clubs were represented at the Twentieth PCI Congress, although their status there was ambiguous. The very value of ritual in marking off those inside and outside the group worked against the continued obfuscation of the boundaries of the new party.

Legitimation and Mystification

Ritual's value in conferring political legitimacy has been appreciated by kings, popes, and rulers of various kinds through the millennia.

The aura of sacrality that people confer on the powerful is nourished and strengthened by ritual performance. By manipulating and claiming ownership of the holy symbols, power holders demonstrate their special status and legitimate their claims to authority. At the same time, ritual vehicles—from inaugurations to imperial processions— guide the contact between the power holders and the masses.

What is it about ritual that gives it this power? Victor Turner draws attention to the way ritual produces certain emotional states and links them with a particular authority structure and view of the world. It is through the "social excitement and directly physiological stimuli" produced by ritual, with its music, singing, and dancing, that, in Turner's view, the "ritual symbol effects an interchange of qualities between its poles of meaning. Norms and values, on the one hand, become saturated with emotion, while the gross and basic emotions become ennobled through contact with social values."[8]

The embarrassing fact is that emotion is as important to political allegiance and political activism as cognition; the genius of ritual lies in fostering heightened emotional states, identifying them both with particular social bonds and with a particular worldview. Ritual propositions are put forth in such a form that they discourage critical inquiry into their message: participation in the rites implies acceptance of the legitimacy of their sponsor. As anthropologist Roy Rappaport states, "Performance of a liturgical order perforce conforms to that order and . . . therefore, authority is intrinsic to liturgy."[9]

Ritual not only legitimizes its sponsors but confers legitimacy on its participants as well. Consider the plight of the heir to the Italian kingdom in the aftermath of World War II. Badly needing to shore up the legitimacy of the monarchy in the wake of its connivance with Mussolini and, later, its cowardly flight in the face of the southward march of the Nazi troops in 1943, Prince Umberto, heir to the throne, sought ritual means of re-legitimation. Opportunity appeared in the form of a demobilization parade of "patriotic" military forces in Milan, scheduled for Sunday, May 6, 1945.

Umberto asked to stand in review of the troops in the parade, thus identifying himself with the anti-Fascist, anti-Nazi forces and showing that the throne represented all Italians, on both Left and Right. Yet leaders of the Resistance forces refused to allow the prince to review their partisan soldiers. Rather than give public symbolic clarity to this rejection, as he would if he were to review only the regular Italian troops, Prince Umberto eschewed the ceremony altogether. A year later a national plebiscite put an end to the Italian monarchy.[10]

As this case shows, the struggle for legitimacy through ritual involves the ability to claim the mantle of particular rituals. The durability of ritual amid the vagaries of political change means that ritual itself becomes a political prize, a kind of holy grail. Political competitors, then, not only fight through ritual but also fight over ritual, that is, over their right to identify with powerful rites.

The dissolution of Communist parties in Eastern Europe has led to widespread battles over the use of alternative rites of legitimation, particularly those associated with religion and nationalism. A good example comes from Poland, where the failing Communist government sought to cloak itself in legitimacy by appropriating powerful rites and symbols of Polish nationalism, from the colors red and white to the use of the image of the Black Madonna of Czestochowa. Yet asserting a claim to sacred symbols and rites does not mean that the claim will be accepted by the intended audience. In this case, the Polish Communists tried and failed.[11]

As for the PCI, it was the old party rituals that helped establish the party's legitimacy and the legitimacy of its leaders. It was the old rituals that gave the party its identity and marked the party off from other political actors. Occhetto and his allies were left in a quandary. They wanted to create a new identity, launch a new political course, yet they could ill afford to relinquish the legitimacy conferred on them by the party's ritual system. Their difficulties were greatly compounded by the fact that their chief rivals, those campaigning against change, were well positioned to maintain their link with the old rituals and, hence, to bolster their own legitimacy at Occhetto's expense.

Solidarity and Ambiguity

By participating together in ritual, people achieve a sense of oneness. The heightening of emotion, the use of various aural and visual stimuli, the chemistry of the crowd, all these give ritual its potency in creating and renewing bonds of solidarity. These are hardly new insights; Durkheim stressed this aspect of ritual at the beginning of the twentieth century.[12]

Less well appreciated is the fact that ritual produces such solidarity without presupposing that the people involved actually interpret the rite in the same way. Communist Party members and sympathizers who assemble in a central piazza, wave red flags, and sing revolutionary songs thereby strengthen their bonds of solidarity with one another and reinforce their sense of identification with the party. While some see the rally as a step toward bringing about the end of capitalism, others view it simply as a pleasant way to spend an evening.[13]

Perhaps the simplest ritual device employed by the Communists for this purpose was the exchange of the term *compagno* among members. In the months of the leadership's struggle over the svolta, it seemed, the more threatened the party's solidarity became, the more incessantly Occhetto invoked the term. Like all party leaders, Occhetto was obliged to begin speeches to the members with the formula "Care compagne e cari compagni" (Dear comrades), thus establishing the solidarity of speaker and audience.[14] In his speeches to various gatherings during the crisis over the party's transformation, however, Occhetto did not limit himself to this prefatory incantation. He began every section of each speech with this ritual appeal to solidarity. This practice reached its height in his opening speech to the Twentieth Party Congress, where the PCI was to be dissolved: Occhetto addressed his audience as "compagni" six times in the concluding section of the speech alone.

Use of *compagno,* together with other ritualized expressions of solidarity, also provided an effective means of linking various unorganized groups to the PCI. In the wake of the 1968 student revolt, for example, the head of the national Communist Youth Federation argued that the student protesters felt close to the PCI. He supported this claim by observing that, in the gatherings of student activists throughout the country, the "chords of the 'Internationale' and the 'Workers' Anthem' ring out, and the students call each other 'compagno' to show that they feel a part of—and that they are in fact an integral part of—the revolutionary workers' movement."[15]

At moments of transition, the use of ritual to produce solidarity becomes especially pronounced, as is reflected in the hyperdevelopment of funerary ritual for fallen political leaders. Stalin's death in 1953 offers a good example of this. An official PCI account of the reaction to the death is revealing:

> In the period between our Seventh National Congress (Rome, April 3–8, 1951) and the current Fourth Conference, a grave, sad loss struck the Communist movement. On March 5, 1953, Comrade Joseph Stalin died, creator with the great Lenin of the October Revolution, who continued Lenin's work, and was the beloved head of the Soviet people and of the revolutionary workers from all corners of the earth. Our party was represented at the solemn ceremonies in Moscow by a delegation headed by the general secretary of the party. Comrade Togliatti himself commemorated him in the Chamber of Deputies [of the Italian parliament], Comrade Scoccimarro in the Senate. Both the House and the Senate recessed after these commemorations in a sign of mourning. A solemn commemorative session of our Party Central Committee was held in Rome. Similar meetings were held in virtually all the provincial capitals of the country, along with thousands of local meetings, open to all citizens, held in sections and cells. Hundreds of thousands of signatures of condolence were gathered by the Communist sections, in books set up for this purpose, and these were all ultimately presented to the Soviet embassy in Italy.[16]

Note first how time is conceived in ritual terms: what marks time are the major public ritual gatherings of the party, the Seventh Party Congress and the Fourth National Party Conference. Throughout this account, *compagno* is used to express not only solidarity but also the official party ideology of equality: compagno Stalin, compagno Togliatti, and compagno Scoccimarro are ritually elevated at the same time as they are ritually leveled.

The rites in the wake of Stalin's death served to express the PCI's solidarity with the Soviet Union and the Soviet Communist Party. Stalin is presented as the leader not only of the USSR but of revolutionary workers everywhere. The PCI's head went to Moscow to propitiate Stalin and the PCI's link to the USSR. By signing a condolence book and then having the books presented to representatives of the USSR, the people are linked to the Soviet Union and its leaders. The PCI's political weight within Italy is expressed by the decision to suspend the sessions of the two chambers of parliament following the eulogies delivered there by the PCI's leaders. Similarly, local meetings of the PCI throughout the country were opened to nonmembers on this occasion in order to promote a larger expression of solidarity with the party.

Ritual Construction of Political Reality

As the case of Stalin's death shows, ritual not only fosters solidarity but also encourages certain views of political reality. It was through ritual, for example, that the view that Soviet Communists, Bulgarian Communists, and Italian Communists were all part of the same movement was most powerfully expressed. Likewise, it was through ritual that the United States could be most effectively identified as the enemy. Togliatti could show the extent of the PCI's loyalty to the Soviet Communist Party through the kinds of rituals previously described. Three decades later, Berlinguer could show the PCI's new distance from the Moscow-directed Communist movement by choosing to spend his summer holiday in China.[17]

Rituals highlight certain events and interpretations and conceal others. A history of the PCI's international position can be read from a history of the public demonstrations that the party has sponsored. It sponsored demonstrations of mourning for Stalin's death, for example, yet none for Mao's. In 1989, a member of the PCI Central Committee, during the CC's initial debate on the svolta, noticed this point. "I had hoped," he declared, "that after the heady days of Berlin the Italian Communists would gather in a large national demonstration to express their joy." Deluded that no such demonstration was ever called, he warned, "Not to have in some way celebrated this victory of ours risks casting a shadow on people's perception of our relation to the upheavals in the East.[18]

The PCI leaders could say all they wanted about how happy they were that the Berlin Wall had fallen, and they could endlessly declare their lack of involvement in the Communist regimes of the East. Yet without proper ritual expression, they were not credible. The PCI had sponsored thousands of demonstrations against the U.S. troops in Vietnam, yet not a single demonstration against Soviet troops in Afghanistan. The party had spoken out against the Soviet invasion of Czechoslovakia, yet had initiated not one public demonstration against it. In this context, when the party sponsored demonstrations in 1989 to protest the Chinese massacre of protesting students in Tiananmen Square, demonstrations in which Occhetto and other party leaders took part, it was clear that a new era was dawning. Ritual speaks much louder than words.

Commemoration of the tenth anniversary of the 1980 Bologna train station bombing, which had killed scores of people, offers a dramatic example of the power of symbolism and ritual to define political reality. In the immediate aftermath of the explosion, with emotions running high, the Communist officials of Bologna identified the authors of the bombing as "Fascists," although no credible claim for the bombing had been made and no evidence identifying the act's perpetrators had come to light. Huge demonstrations were organized in Bologna, channeling popular rage over the massacre into an expression of solidarity around the PCI and city officials. These rites afforded the local officials powerful occasions for speaking out on behalf of the population against the evil in their midst. The ritual commemorations of the tenth anniversary of the explosion were challenged, however, by leaders of the Movimento Sociale Italiano. In response to a request by a Communist deputy in the national parliament for a moment of silence to mark the occasion, the MSI called for a parliamentary order to change the wording on the commemorative plaque found in Bologna's main piazza. In particular, the MSI demanded that reference to Fascist responsibility for the bombing be removed from the plaque, which had been placed at the center of a shrine erected to the victims of the bombing. To the anger of the Communists, the Christian Democratic prime minister, Giulio Andreotti, agreed, and heated debate about the proper ritualization of the bombing followed.

The leader of the PCI parliamentary delegation, Giulio Quercini, argued that even though the individuals involved in the bombing had not been discovered, "in any event the nature, the method, and the anti-democratic purpose" of the action "is Fascist." He concluded gravely, "The president of the council [that is, the prime minister] could not find a worse way on this day of the tenth anniversary of the massacre to wound the memory of the victims and the democratic sensibilities of the Bolognese community and of all Italians."[19]

The Communist newspaper, *L'Unità,* reported that in response to the MSI parliamentary proposal, thousands of people gathered before the shrine in Bologna's central piazza. Their reaction to the request to remove the term *fascista* from the plaque was, the paper reported, "Anger, stupor, and again anger." "Shameful" is how the head of Bologna's PCI Federation labeled the suggestion. At the same time, the head of the organization of relatives of the bombing victims announced, "We will defend that plaque and keep it as it is. And we will consider all those who have paid heed to Rauti's request [Rauti being the notorious leader of the extremist wing of the MSI] to be friends of the Fascists."[20]

In battling over symbols, ritual is clearly a potent weapon. It assigns a particular meaning to the symbols, thereby fixing the symbolic definition of reality, while equating one's own political group with good and the other with evil. Such ritual offensives are often met by counter-offensives, most effectively in the form of counter-ritual. On the surface, this is simply a matter of each side's trying to undermine the ritual claim being made by the other. A kind of collaboration between the two sides is often evident, however. Each side needs, on one hand, a personification of evil, and, on the other, a means of emotionally activating and demarcating its own group. This can be accomplished through the kind of direct symbolic combat that ritual makes possible.

A dramatic example of such combat over the definition of political reality took place in connection with the Triangle of Death polemics examined in Chapter 6. Although the party responded to the charges that the PCI and Togliatti had been complicit in the killings following Liberation in 1945—through a raft of denunciatory press releases and interviews—its most effective response was via ritual. Only through ritual could party leaders effectively assert their claim to be speaking for a greater mass of people; at the same time such public ritual could whip up the emotions of the members and sympathizers in a way that other forms of communication could not. In the midst of the polemics, party leaders announced that a national demonstration would be held in Reggio Emilia, at the heart of the Triangle of Death, where all party forces—regardless of their division over the svolta—would come together "in defense of the Liberation struggle."[21]

For its part, the MSI could not pass up the symbolic possibilities offered by the occasion, and it promptly announced that it would hold its own national conference and procession in Reggio Emilia on the same day. The ritual battle was joined; its tenor is reflected in the breathless account that was published in L'Unità on the morning of the confrontation:

Reggio Emilia. It is a bitter day that Reggio will live today. In the afternoon, in a downtown hotel, the Fascists will hold a conference to hail "the truth that everyone knows about the Triangle of Death," a gathering that ANPI [the national partisans' association] has defined as a "provocation," CGIL [the PCI-allied national trade union confederation] has called "contemptible," and the PCI has labeled "dismal." And at the exact same time, just a few hundred meters away, in the piazza named for the martyrs of July 7, 1960, the partisans will gather in silence, under the portrait of Alcide Cervi, in front of the bronze plaque on which the names of his seven sons are engraved along with the other six hundred sons of this land who fell in the Resistance.

Joining the partisans will be a silent crowd of citizens, of union activists, of youths and workers, indignant at the presence in their city—a gold-medal city of the Resistance—of the heirs of a violent and bloody past, and indignant at the defamatory campaign that their presence is aimed at promoting. ANPI's demonstration will be silent; the only speech will be provided by the names of those dead [listed on the plaque], both their real names and their nicknames, and of the tiny photos beside each name.[22]

The wealth of symbolism employed here, and activated through ritual, is overwhelming, mixing a certain interpretation of history with the power to stir deep emotions, create solidarity, and confer legitimacy.

The ritual served, first of all, to define and legitimize the PCI. The PCI was defined in part through the identification of its enemy, the fascisti. The party of 1990 was ritually transposed through time to refight the battle against the Nazis and Fascists of the mythic Resistance. The setting—Reggio Emilia—entered into hagiography through a series of ritual means: the city was cited for its gold medal (awarded to cities where the Resistance was fought); the central piazza, strewn with red roses and carnations, was named for the

fallen martyrs of the anti-Fascist demonstrations in 1960; the partigiani marched holding aloft a portrait of Alcide Cervi, whose seven
sons had been executed by the Nazis. They proceeded silently—
recalling a religious procession, with its sanctified mood—to the
shrine with the names and tiny pictures of the Resistance martyrs.
Only two other organizations were symbolically represented: the
PCI-linked national labor federation and the national partisans' association. Shortly after the official procession passed, demonstrators
from the extreme leftist Proletarian Democracy Party marched by,
ritually exhibiting their militancy by chanting such old favorites as
"Comrade with the black beret, you belong in the cemetery" (Cam-
erata basco nero, il tuo posto è il cimitero).[23]

Meanwhile, the MSI held its conference concerning the facts of
the Triangle of Death in a nearby hotel in the center of the city. Large
numbers of anti-Fascist demonstrators gathered outside, with riot-
equipped police stationed to keep the ritual combatants apart. When
the MSI members began to leave the hotel and enter the piazza, the
ritual battle ensued. The MSI contingent was immediately greeted
with whistles, shouts, and slogans from the crowd. The *missini*
reacted by giving Roman salutes, their arms outstretched before
them, and launched into songs of the Fascist yesteryear. In the anti-
Fascist crowd, youths showed their militancy by placing red ban-
dannas around their faces, while others met the Fascist songs with
louder songs of the Resistance. As some of the bandanna-clad youths
gathered rocks, the police moved in to disperse them. Just a few
meters away, at the shrine to the Resistance in the central piazza, the
partisans' association continued its vigil.[24]

The instructional value of this ritual battle for the PCI was much
on the minds of party leaders. The day after the confrontation, the
party's provincial head for Reggio Emilia explained that the events
had had a positive effect: "These days in Reggio there is perhaps a
new generation of youths—both Communist and not—youths who
are disenchanted, ecologists, pacifists, nonviolent—who are learning
in a new way to love the Resistance."[25]

Party Congresses

Except during the Fascist period, when they were suppressed, national party congresses were the PCI's holiest rite. They defined the party organization through a series of symbolic presentations of the structure of leadership and by linking members to the party through a capillary procedure of preparatory local-level meetings that elected delegates to higher levels. They legitimized the party leaders and their political line by providing a mechanism to demonstrate the support of the membership, and by identifying the leaders with the holy symbols of the party. The party congresses increased the solidarity of the members, whose bonds were renewed through the panoply of rites surrounding the congresses. The structure of symbols bound up in the ritual defined who were friends and who enemies, and provided a template for understanding the nature of world and national events.

In this light, it is not surprising that party congresses were major battlefields in the efforts to transform the PCI into the PDS. Party congresses were required to enable Occhetto to legitimize the new party as the heir of the old, while defining it in a new way. At the same time, in the heightened emotional context of such powerful rites, the opposition was given an important opportunity to assert its own claims to legitimacy and promulgate its own construction of political reality.

The use of party congressional ritual in 1990–91, though, can only be understood in the context of the national PCI congresses that preceded it. The congresses had acquired a certain ritual grammar, which the contestants for power had to heed.

Just as the first congresses had offered the party its most powerful means to identify with the Bolshevik Revolution, postwar congresses became major opportunities for the PCI to express its solidarity with the regimes of the Soviet bloc and to identify this bloc with peace and prosperity. Indeed, for the first three decades following the war, representatives of the Communist Parties of Eastern

Europe were honored guests at the congresses, and their speeches of solidarity and fraternal greeting were liberally sprinkled throughout the gatherings.

The Seventh Party Congress, held in Rome in 1951, offers a graphic example. The Communist mayor of Bologna, taking the chair for the opening ceremonies, began by warmly greeting the Communist Party of the Soviet Union and its "great leader Stalin." He then proceeded to read a telegram from the Central Committee of the Soviet Communist Party addressed to the congress, in which the Soviet Communist Party sent "its fraternal greeting to the Seventh Congress of the PCI, leader of the working class and of all Italian workers." The delegates responded, according to the official party account, with "long applause and a great ovation for the Communist Party of the USSR and for Stalin." The stage was then set for the lengthy opening address by party head Palmiro Togliatti.[26]

In 1951, attention was focused on the city of Trieste, which, in the wake of the war, still remained under Allied control. The appearance of Vittorio Vidali, the head of the Communist Party of Trieste, took on considerable symbolic significance. Reflecting the times, Vidali concluded his speech to the congress with the ritual incantation "Viva the Italian Communist Party and its great leader Palmiro Togliatti! And viva proletarian internationalism! Viva the Soviet Union, bulwark of world peace! Viva our beloved teacher and head, Comrade Stalin!" As he stepped down, the delegates rose in a prolonged ovation.[27]

Such party congresses also served to legitimize the party and its leadership through constant use of Resistance symbolism and martyrology. Taking advantage of the symbolic possibilities offered by the congress's location in Rome, the party leadership at the seventh congress proposed from the podium that a delegation representing the congress be commissioned to lay wreaths at the grave of Antonio Gramsci and at the shrine at Fosse Ardeatine. (The latter site, where, in 1944, Nazi troops had taken scores of Roman civilians and executed them, remains a major center for ritual activity.) Later, the congress was addressed by the widow of a revered Communist who had been martyred at the Mathausen concentration camp. And, just after the last regular speech at the congress, a group of gold-medal winners came to the podium. They were described as follows: "The partisan commander Arrigo Boldrini announces at the microphone that, expressing the thoughts of all the Garibaldi volunteers who fought in Spain, Garibaldian gold medals will be awarded in memory of the Spanish [Civil] War to combatants for liberty Togliatti, Longo, Fischer, Vidali."[28]

The congresses provided a valuable mechanism for dividing the world into the good and the bad, and in the process defining the "us" and the "them." By the late 1960s, "us" included not only the other Communist parties of the world, especially of the Soviet bloc, but the "national liberation movements" of the third world as well.

Typical of this use of symbolism was the 1971 FGCI national congress. The congress started off with the words "We salute the youth organizations of all the fraternal Communist Parties both from the socialist countries and from those countries that, like ours, are still engaged in the struggle to defeat capitalism." The chair continued, "We greet the youth organizations of all the national liberation movements, which have come here from all the countries of Latin America, Asia, Africa, all of the world engaged in the struggle against imperialism."[29]

This kind of ritual permitted symbolic identifications that could not be easily made in other ways because they did not correspond to the actual policy of the party. The implication—that the PCI was working day and night to overthrow capitalism and join the ranks of the countries ruled by the "fraternal Communist Parties" of the socialist countries—was far from accurate in describing what the party leaders were doing.

Near the end of the 1971 FGCI congress, Enrico Berlinguer, then second in command of the PCI, gave a major address. Again, the emphasis was on the division of the world into two camps, and here the rites were used self-consciously to create solidarity:

We express our solidarity with you, comrades of the Soviet Union and the socialist countries, with you, comrades and friends from the national liberation movements, with you, comrades who struggle, as we do, in the capitalist countries, with you, comrades of Spain, Greece, and Portugal, who battle to free yourselves from shameful Fascist dictatorships; it is a solidarity that today makes us feel as brothers, above all, with our comrades of Vietnam, Laos, and Cambodia, who battle in the most advanced trenches of the anti-imperialist struggle, and to our Palestinian comrades and patriots who, with their sacrifices and their victories, are giving an incalculable and powerful aid to all peoples and to our people.[30]

By sitting in a convention hall in Italy, the young Communist could thus become one with the fighters against evil throughout the world.

Sanctioning the Svolta: The Nineteenth Party Congress

In the wake of Occhetto's November 1989 announcement of the svolta, and his clear majority in the subsequent meeting of the Central Committee, the "extraordinary" party congress seemed to offer the opposition its only hope of defeating the post-Communist movement. But the majority could use the holding of a congress, the party's principal ritual, to legitimize the svolta, retain party solidarity, and define a new political reality for member and nonmember alike. The trick for Occhetto's forces would be to use the grammar of past party congresses to combine the old and the new.

The process began, as for previous congresses, with local party section meetings called throughout the country for members to debate the proposals before the congress, vote on them, and elect representatives to the next higher body, the federation (or provincial-level) gatherings, which would repeat the procedure, ultimately producing eleven hundred delegates to the national congress.

All told, 400,000 of the 1.4 million party members cast votes in often stormy local section meetings; 66 percent voted in favor of

Occhetto's proposal (Motion 1), and most of the rest (31 percent) for the main opposition motion (Motion 2). The third motion, identified with hard-line Communist Armando Cossutta, received only 3 percent of the ballots. Occhetto had a clear majority, but never before had there been a PCI congress with such a large and well-organized faction publicly dedicated to opposing the party head's program.[31]

Occhetto and his allies sought to use the congress to transform the party's symbolism, but in doing so they faced an opposition intent on using the power of that symbolism against them. As the congress opened, the majority's symbolic strategy was evident in the decorations of the Palazzo dello Sport, where the national congress was held. Displays of the word *Communism* were absent, and the central party icon, the hammer and sickle, was shrunk to practically microscopic size. The rousing slogans and banners that had decorated past party congresses were missing; the single slogan on display was simply the ambiguous "For a New Phase of the Left."

The one traditional symbol that remained was the color red, which indeed dominated the proceedings: the massive steplike staging area at the front of the hall, on which the party leaders sat and from which speakers addressed the delegates, was entirely red. As the congress got under way, though, a telltale change became clear: unlike past congresses, no foreign delegations had been invited to this one. Representatives of "fraternal" Communist parties had now become an embarrassment, their solidarity no longer ritually desirable.

As it turned out, Occhetto and his allies were not fully up to the challenge of competing with the minority on the rich symbolic terrain of a national party congress. While abandoning many of the symbols and rites that had given past PCI congresses their identity, and which had bound the members to the congressional activities, the leaders of the majority lacked any powerful new symbolism to replace the old. They proposed no new party name, no new symbol, no new song, nor any new rites for expressing party identity or membership solidarity with the party. All the rites and symbols of solidarity, legitimacy, and identity were the old rites, which had now become identified with the opposition.

Tension was in the air as delegates gathered in Bologna for the dramatic nineteenth congress. The day before the congress opened, a young bellboy at a Bologna hotel went to help an older client bring his bags into the lobby. The bellboy greeted him by observing that he must be in town for the Communist Party congress. Yes, the older man replied, but how did you know? Because, the bellboy responded, you look like a Communist. Oblivious to the older man's distress, the youth added his own political analysis: that is one of the reasons the PCI is having problems, he said, you can tell a Communist by the way he looks. At this, the man raised up his arms in exasperation and exclaimed, "Then it isn't enough to change our name, we also have to change our face?"[32]

When the congress began, it was clear that the basic PCI congressional structure had not changed. The congress opened and closed with long speeches by the party head, with scores of short speeches by party delegates sandwiched in between. Occhetto's problems were clear from the beginning: his opening three-hour speech engendered little more than respectful applause among the restive delegates. The potent symbols that had roused congress audiences in the past were largely lacking. Indeed, the first interruption for applause came twenty minutes into the speech, when Occhetto invoked the sacred names of Nelson Mandela and Daniel Ortega. The next applause was heard when he praised the heroic struggle of the Palestinian people. In short, that part of his speech that invoked the standard party icons, that remained within the hallowed ritual frame, allowed the delegates to transport themselves into special, ritual time. By contrast, his explanation for dropping traditional party symbols and changing the party's identity, and his criticism of the parties of Eastern Europe, were met with profound unease.

At the conclusion of the opening address, ritual form called for the other party leaders, assembled around the party secretary on the congressional altar, to rise in enthusiastic standing applause. A powerful message was sent when conferees saw former secretary Alessandro Natta get up with evident reluctance, Cossutta keep his hands resolutely at his side, and both Pietro Ingrao and Lucio Magri go to great lengths to affect a lack of interest in what was going on around them.[33]

Leaders of the opposition, by contrast, were well positioned to take advantage of the symbolic forum offered by the congress. In the session following the secretary's uninspiring speech, Pietro Ingrao, leader of the "no" forces, denounced the svolta. As he concluded his remarks, his supporters leaped to their feet to sing "Bandiera rossa" and the "Internationale." The prolonged display of emotion proved a bitter trial for Occhetto who, after polite applause, remained disconsolately perched over a crowd that had exploded in joyful celebration. Other party leaders went up to shake Ingrao's hand, but Occhetto remained in his seat, wincing as the crowd bellowed "Pie-TRO! Pie-TRO!"

By the time Occhetto returned to the podium for the concluding speech on the last day of the congress, he was clearly on the defensive. He could say nothing critical about the history of the PCI, nothing to mar the holy symbolism of the party. He mentioned the Soviet Union only in a positive vein, to congratulate Gorbachev (although he no longer referred to him as "Comrade" Gorbachev). He never mentioned the United States except to criticize it. In short, in warding off the attacks of the opposition, he sought to locate himself on the party's familiar symbolic terrain.

The most effective part of his speech was undoubtedly, and not coincidentally, the words with which he concluded, a passage devoted almost entirely to the symbology of the party:

> Some observers have noted that the hall of the congress is, this time, especially red. Let me say right away that this by no means contrasts with the course on which we are set. Red is the color of the workers' movement of socialist and Communist inspira-

tion. At the end of the congresses of the Socialist International, "Red Flag" is sung in Italian, the same as happens in Moscow. It is the sign of a common, glorious heritage, which we certainly do not renounce. We want to change many things, but we do not intend to leave the historical ground from which we have sprung.[34]

On the defensive, and with the power of the traditional party rites and symbols painfully on display at the congress, Occhetto retreated, re-embracing the old party rituals and providing a historical rationale for why such symbolic continuity was not, as it appeared, inconsistent with his plan to drop the old party name. Members could keep most of their old icons (only the term *Communist* and the hammer and sickle were to be discouraged), their old songs and colors, and could continue to call one another "compagno."

Occhetto's successful use of the party's symbols, combined with the need the delegates felt to express party solidarity in the face of uncertainty, produced a warm reaction to his speech. At its conclusion, the audience stood, applauding, as the party secretary was brought first one, then a second bouquet of red roses. His most implacable adversaries showed their opposition by refusing to applaud, attempting to feign a lack of interest in the pandemonium below them.

The dramatic highlight of this concluding rite came when Pietro Ingrao, elder statesman of the opposition, moved across the platform to shake Occhetto's hand and briefly embrace him. This prompted thunderous applause, punctuated by shrieks of approval. From the crowd of delegates arose the strains of "Bandiera rossa," which gathered force to become a booming, stirring chorus, accompanied by a thousand pairs of hands beating in rhythmic applause. A thousand voices brought the song to an end with the emphatic (if soon to be anachronistic) line, "evviva il comunismo e la libertà." Thus aroused, delegates bellowed the "Internationale," thrusting their right fists above their heads in periodic punctuation.

Yet, paradoxically, Occhetto's apparent victory in fact amounted to a setback. The emotional reaction to his speech revealed more about the hold of the old party symbols and rites than it reflected any enthusiasm for the changes he proposed. In this sense, the remarks of Luigi Pintor, exponent of the left-wing Manifesto group that opposed Occhetto, are apt: "The opponents . . . counted more than the victors in this congress and leave it politically better off."[35] Luciana Castellina, a member of the party's Central Committee, explained, "The emotion and applause for Ingrao the other evening are an important political fact. While I looked around the hall I asked myself what an absurdity it would be to dissolve this extraordinary political force." She went on, "It is revealing that the moment of the greatest real enthusiasm at the congress came, following Occhetto's concluding address, when people sang "Bandiera rossa" as they watched Occhetto and Ingrao embrace." In accordance with the Communists' traditional delegitimation of any argument based on the role of emotion, Castellina concluded defensively, "These are not emotional facts; they must be taken into account."[36]

The Death of a Communist

In the liminal period between the nineteenth and twentieth party congresses, with party symbols in flux and the comrades' sense of identity threatened, rituals of solidarity offered welcome emotional release and reassurance. Such rites—bringing party members to-gether under the old symbols, renewing their bonds of solidarity, reinvigorating their construction of history, and legitimizing the party leadership—could no longer be combined, as in the past, with regular programmatic activities. The party congresses, which had always served these purposes, were now factional battlegrounds.

What remained was death, which, as before, provided a way to create a sacred time linking past to present. It was the death of a Com-munist that would, for a fleeting but exalting time, allow party mem-bers to enter into a kind of communion that would soon be lost to them.

On September 14, 1990, Italians read in their morning newspapers of the death of Giancarlo Pajetta, the seventy-nine-year-old
legendary Communist Party leader. Pajetta embodied much of the
mythic structure of the PCI, and, as more than one observer noted,
his death seemed symbolically appropriate, foreshadowing the
demise of his beloved party.

Pajetta, one of the last survivors of the Resistance leadership and
one of the few surviving members of the party leadership from the
Fascist period, had become the symbolic embodiment of the party's
identification with the anti-Fascist struggle and the Resistance. The
party's efforts to link these earlier anti-Fascist battles with its postwar activities through military metaphor found in Pajetta the perfect vehicle.

Appropriately, the banner headline announcing Pajetta's death
in *L'Unità* read, "Pajetta, the great rebel, died at age 79, battling to
the end." The piece continued, "Italy and the PCI mourn Giancarlo
Pajetta, the mythical Commander 'Nullo' of the Resistance." And, lest
the point be lost, the opening paragraph proclaimed, "And so, at age
79, has died Giancarlo Pajetta, the 'red boy,' one of the symbols of the
Resistance and of the PCI." This was immediately followed by Achille
Occhetto's comment, "We salute him not only for his role as PCI
combatant but as the man of the Resistance and of the anti-Fascist
battle." The military struggle against Mussolini and Hitler, in short,
had never come to an end; the PCI continued to fight over the following half century.[37]

Lest anyone not already be familiar with the mythic contours of
Pajetta's life, a full page hagiography appeared in the same issue of
L'Unità. The extended headline summed up the main elements: "The
death of the red boy. At just age fourteen his encounter with the PCI.
The first struggles, the trip to Moscow and a decade in prison. Orga-
nizer and director of the partisan movement in the north. His criticisms of Togliatti in '56 for [Togliatti's] cautiousness on Stalinism,
which he later called his 'impatience.' The solitude of a man who saw
himself as constituting the 'faction of those against factions.'"

Pajetta retained the sobriquet of "ragazzo rosso" at age seventy-nine because he had first been arrested for PCI-related anti-Fascist activities at fourteen. Indeed, one of the best-known stories about him involved a childhood bout with political ritual: at age sixteen, it is said, he was ejected from public school for refusing to return his teachers' Roman salute. Although he spent time in Moscow in the early 1930s as a representative of the FGCI, the only way in which he is tied to Stalinism or the USSR in his obituary is his supposed impatience with PCI foot-dragging in denouncing Stalin in 1956. Most of all, having spent ten years in prison for anti-Fascist activities and having then become a leader of the Resistance forces, Pajetta is repeatedly referred to as "Comandante Nullo," a nom de guerre borrowed from one of Garibaldi's mythic "thousand."[38] Finally, the reference to his comment about being the only member of the party's faction against having factions alludes to the use recently made of him in the party as symbol of the supreme value of the unity of the party, opponent of those who threatened a schism.

Only a few days before his death, Pajetta had been dispatched north to join the symbolic battle over the Triangle of Death. His major appearance of the trip was, appropriately, at a meeting held at the Milan headquarters of the partisans' veterans association. The symbolic juxtaposition that resulted was noted not only by the Communist press but by other journalists as well: "At the time 'Comandante Nullo' arrived, the [provincial] headquarters of the National Partisans Association had become the target of the neo-Fascists." The article went on to describe the scene: "The large front windows had been smashed, the showcases with the announcements of the commemorative events had been destroyed. The place was covered with spray-painted swastikas and insults directed at the Resistance." The picture accompanying the article showed the outside wall of the Milan ANPI headquarters with a spray-painted swastika and, in large letters, "Partigiani assassini."[39]

On the morning of September 14, Pajetta's coffin—covered by the red flag of his local party section—was placed on view in the rotunda of the PCI headquarters in Rome. Thousands of party members filed by, some of the older ones with their fists raised, tears streaming down their faces. In the afternoon the funeral procession began, bearing the coffin on a route from the national party headquarters on via Botteghe Oscure to the piazza facing the parliament building where Pajetta had, for decades, served as PCI deputy. The notes of the "Internationale" were played to a slow, funereal beat; the banners of the gold-medal cities of the Resistance, borne by delegations of partisans, led the march. Banners proclaiming "Addío partigiano Nullo" and "Viva the glorious Resistance" dotted the throng. Along the way, a reporter for *L'Unità* recounted, an eighty-two-year-old woman wandered by herself. She had, alone, left her retirement home in Istria—hundreds of kilometers to the north—in order to take part, saying simply, "I have always been a Communist. . . . I couldn't fail to say goodbye to Pajetta." A woman next to her was overheard telling a friend, "Well, now they'll have to speak well of the Resistance."[40]

Indeed, the funeral procession was pervaded with Resistance symbolism, and Resistance songs filled the air. Among the speakers was the national president of ANPI, along with Ottaviano Del Turco, national leader of the CGIL—and a Socialist—who reduced many to tears as he recalled what it meant for a young lad like Pajetta to spend his entire youth in prison.

Occhetto, meanwhile, was in a delicate but potentially advantageous position. He could improve his position through the rite, but to do so he had to ensure that nothing in his remarks be seen as divisive or self-serving. His central task was to identify himself with Pajetta and with the symbolism surrounding him, thereby profiting from the power of the emotions generated by the ceremonies. As he spoke to the crowd in the piazza, he turned to Pajetta's family. Speaking in a voice cracking with emotion, he told them of their importance to the nation's history. He praised the courage of Pajetta's mother, Elvira, who, in addition to seeing Giancarlo imprisoned, saw another son killed by the Fascists and a third deported and tortured by the Nazis.

It was, proclaimed Occhetto, a moment for party unity. Sadly noting Pajetta's own anguish at the crisis that had overtaken the party, and alluding respectfully to Pajetta's disagreement with him on the proper direction for the party's future, Occhetto concluded, "I believe that even if the vision of the party that we have today differs from that which men like Pajetta, who were molded in an iron age, had . . . we can't help but appreciate and interpret, in the light of our own experience, that value of unity which they so vigorously affirmed."

The funeral ceremony—televised live to the nation—concluded with the playing once again of the "Internationale." The red flag–draped coffin, red roses strewn atop, made its way out of the piazza, as thousands held their fists above their head and proudly raised their voices in Communist communion, singing "Bella ciao" and "Bandiera rossa."

The End of the PCI: The Twentieth Party Congress

Occhetto had hoped to have a single congress sanction the proposed svolta and give birth to the new party, but the opposition forced him to devote a second special congress to the task. As Occhetto portrayed it, the purpose of the twentieth congress was not to debate the direction the party was heading in, for this is what the nineteenth congress had been all about. Rather, it was, he argued, simply a formal matter of inaugurating the new political formation and making the official transition from the PCI to the new entity. Yet the opposition took a very different position, which in fact set the agenda for the twentieth congress. In their view, because the nineteenth congress had not been presented with any concrete plan for a new party (or new political formation), it had not been in a position to approve one. Hence the question of the conservation of the Communist identity of the party remained open, and the twentieth congress, being a sovereign body of the PCI, had full power to reconsider the direction approved at the nineteenth. Thus in the months leading up to the twentieth congress, while Occhetto and his allies developed and announced the new name and emblem of the party—the PDS, with its rugged oak tree—they had to fend off attacks from the minority.

The twentieth congress, held ten months after the nineteenth in the Adriatic coastal city of Rimini, took place in what was not only a period of great internal party anguish but one of unusual international tension as well. The American-led allied assault on Iraqi troops in Kuwait and Iraq had begun only days earlier. Revealingly, Occhetto's forces, who might have voiced support for the military expulsion of Iraqi troops from Kuwait as a way of demonstrating the new international collocation they sought, instead fell back on old rhetoric and old symbols. It was judged more important to fend off the threatened schism of the anti-reformists within the party than to send a signal of a change in the nature of the party to the outside.[41]

In his opening speech to the delegates who were to give birth to the new party and presumably (although he could not admit it) bring about the death of the old, Occhetto spent his first half hour denouncing American military intervention. In his only concession to the new party-building task before him, rather than justify his stance by citing the Soviet Union or imperialism, he approvingly instead cited the pope and offered an essentially pacifistic rationale. In short, opposition to the U.S. military became the means for constructing solidarity in the fractious party, while burnishing Occhetto's leftist credentials in the face of his enemies' charge that he was no better than a Social Democrat.

The symbolic structure of the twentieth congress reflected an attempt to reinforce the sagging solidarity of the old party, combined with an attempt to demonstrate what was supposed to be the novelty of the new party: the inclusion of pacifists, environmentalists, Catholic leftists, and assorted others. The resulting mixture of symbols was not entirely successful.

In deference to the old, the congress began with the playing of the "Internationale," followed by the showing of a series of videos on a huge electronic screen dangling over the convention hall. The video began with a scene from Pajetta's speech to the previous fall's festa dell'Unità, superimposed with huge letters reading "Thank you Comrade Pajetta." A video history of the PCI then followed, leading into the pacifistic picture of youths singing "All we are saying is give peace a chance" (in English). At the last "All we are saying . . . " the lights over the platform gradually brightened and the formal program began.

The hall's decorations reflected the transitional nature of the proceedings. The stage was draped in red, but the podium and the tables for the delegates were covered in green, recalling the wooing of environmentalists. Use of the green also enabled an alternative interpretation of the red, for green and red (and white) are the colors of the Italian flag. A PCI emblem was affixed to one side of the stage, but it was balanced by the new PDS emblem on the other side. Above hung not a party name or slogan but, rather, a single word, "Twentieth," written in highly stylized script.

Occhetto's opening speech likewise wove symbolic claims of continuity with the past—which prompted enthusiasm in the audience—with assorted references to the new—which did not. His calls for an end to NATO as a military alliance drew applause, as did his mention of the recent celebration of Gramsci's hundredth birthday. Indeed, he repeatedly invoked Gramsci to legitimize and express continuity: "We will carry Gramsci with us in the new party."[42] By contrast, his repeated allusions to the pope, and to the need for an environmental movement, drew a tepid response at best.

The following day the congress began with another symbolic gesture of continuity, as the chair read a telegram from Gorbachev on behalf of the Communist Party of the USSR. There followed the speech of Aldo Tortorella, representing the moderate opposition. He, too, began by spending twenty minutes denouncing the military operation led by the United States in the Persian Gulf, expressing satisfaction that the party stood together on this issue. A wave of applause greeted his invocation of each of the litany of sacred symbols in the PCI repertoire: Panama, Nicaragua, Grenada, Palestinian Liberation Organization, Intifada, and the new "withdrawal of the Italian ships and troops" from the Gulf.

In an emotional conclusion, Tortorella fervently swore that he would never stop feeling himself to be a Communist but added that nonetheless he was against secession. Roaring applause greeted this dual profession of faith. He ended by praising the PCI's "noble past" as his sympathizers rose in applause.

Intense interest was also aroused by the speech of Armando Cossutta, leader and symbol of the philo-Soviet opposition to Occhetto. His comments in the months leading to the twentieth congress, declaring the inevitability of a schism should the majority have its way, had prompted consternation in the party. Like his predecessors, Cossutta began his remarks by attacking the United States, accused of mounting an "infernal war machine, entirely disproportionate" to the situation. It was a military action aimed, he decried, at imposing "American hegemony in the entire region, and on a worldwide scale," motivated among other reasons by the desire to "give a further blow to the remaining international prestige of the USSR."[43]

Cossutta stressed the link between the members' personal identity and the Communist identity of the party, offering his own credentials as party high priest. "I have been in the party since 1943, and I have dedicated my entire life to this party, from prison to the Resistance to the countless battles covering almost a half century, I have known great sacrifices." He had no wish to break up the party, he declared, but thundered, in a familiar refrain, "you cannot prevent me from remaining Communist . . . nor can you stop my children."[44]

chapter eight

On the Power of Symbols
and the Weight of History

Symbolism in Politics

At the heart of mass politics in modern societies is the ability of elites to create groups, that is, to get a significant number of people to conceive of themselves as belonging to some group that the leader represents. In Foucault's terms, to understand the wielding of power, we need to understand how people come to select certain identities for themselves.[1] These identities take shape and are maintained through a constant process of symbolic struggle, either in shoring up an existing symbolic universe or in attempting to change it.

Yet a nagging doubt remains: are elites free to produce any symbolic offerings they like? Is there not something "out there in the real world" that affects their success in promulgating these representations? Bourdieu, whose writings on politics and symbolism I looked at earlier, is rather fuzzy on this point. After stating that the most exemplary form of symbolic power is the "power to produce groups," he identifies the two variables that affect the leader's success in this process as: (1) the possession of "symbolic capital," that is, "social authority acquired in previous struggles"; and (2) the "degree to which the vision proposed is based on reality." Bourdieu goes on to specify: "Symbolic power is a power of creating things with words. It is only if it is true, that is, adequate to things, that a description can create things."[2]

We are thus brought back to the hard surface of "reality," to the commonsense notion that there are in fact "things" out there to which our symbols must relate. Yet how we can reach this level remains unclear. For Foucault, of course, "truth" is itself to be understood as a function of power; he speaks of a "regime" of truth.[3]

Neither Bourdieu's nor Foucault's formulations seem entirely adequate. There is indeed a material world, which exists independently of the symbolic webs that we spin to represent it. Yet our political world, most of the time, bears only indirectly on this material world, so that in most cases our symbolic constructions are not directly verifiable or falsifiable through reference to the touchstone of material reality.

What of the notion that the symbolic and ritual dimension of politics should be distinguished from that of the "real," that symbols are the fluff of politics, while policies and "practice" are the reality? The case of the PCI presents us with many examples that analysts of this persuasion might use to make their point. For instance, whereas in terms of policy, of votes in parliament, and of work on parliamentary committees, the PCI had long embraced capitalism, the symbolism of the party was overwhelmingly anti-capitalist, and ritual denunciations of the evils of capitalism were regularly proclaimed. Likewise, it could be argued, while Communism was symbolically glorified, in practice it was rejected.

These facts lend themselves to different interpretations. The anthropologist Maurice Bloch, studying the evolution of politics and society in Madagascar over some centuries, was struck by how stable the symbolism and ritual were during a time of great political and economic change. More to our point, he found that the same symbolism and the same rites continued to be used by elites to shore up their power, even as the political system changed. Given our view of such rites and symbols as providing people with their identity and giving them a sense of continuity, this should not be surprising.[4]

My objection to viewing such cases in terms of a contrast between the symbolic and the real is that the real in fact involves the manipulation of symbols as much as the symbolic, and the symbolic itself is not without its material consequences. A neat contrast between what a politician or political group says and does has appeal in terms of puncturing political hypocrisy, but as a theory of politics, or a theory of culture, it is naive.

In looking at the case of the terminal crisis of the Italian Communist Party, I have emphasized the ways in which the symbols that represent political entities, such as parties, draw their strength by simultaneously representing individuals. One might say that individuals use these symbols to represent themselves to themselves as well as to others. As anthropologist James Fernandez remarked, we need to objectify ourselves, just as we need to objectify others.[5]

Various philosophers, psychologists, and historians have come to similar conclusions, focusing in particular on the way people produce narratives about themselves. In this view, for people to have a coherent sense of self, they must somehow (generally implicitly and unconsciously) create a narrative of their lives. That is, they give their lives a meaning by giving them a narrative structure. Husserl, along these lines, wrote that the person "constitutes itself for itself, so to speak, in the unity of a *Geschichte,*" that is, a history, or a story. Citing this passage, David Carr writes that we constitute ourselves by giving ourselves a history through the unity of a story we make up about ourselves.[6] Carr suggests that we are constantly engaged in autobiographical revision, that our unity of self is achieved only through constant effort.

Maintaining or restoring narrative coherence involves the constant struggle against chaos. It is a battle, in Carr's view, that takes two forms: (1) we fit the pieces of life, as we confront them, into the framework of our already formed narrative; and (2) when it becomes difficult to fit the pieces into the story, we change the narrative. Viewed in this light, the history of the PCI until 1989 was the history of fitting the pieces into an already formed narrative; what Occhetto proposed in that year was that the narrative itself change and, with it, the identity and the history of those who had based their personal narratives on it.[7]

Personal identity, in this perspective, is a process. We make sense of the social and political world around us by a process of categorization that assigns individuals to a given set of identities. In order to be able to simplify the social world around us so drastically, we must make use of a limited repertoire of symbols.[8]

Occhetto's efforts recall Bourdieu's "oracle effect," which "enables the authorized spokesperson to take his authority from the group which authorizes him in order to exercise recognized constraint, symbolic violence, on each of the isolated members of the group."[9] In divining a new future, Occhetto called on his following to create a new past.

Although I have emphasized the battle between elites within the PCI in their struggle over control of the future of the party, the mass of members clearly also played a role in determining the party's fate. Occhetto's inability to move the members as quickly and as forcefully as he would have liked emboldened the opposition elites—who, of course, did all they could to stoke membership opposition—and led to a result quite different from his goal. The inherent conservatism of symbols and rites fed members' resistance to the changes Occhetto championed.

Politics and Rational Action

The view of politics I have been championing challenges a rational action (or, in the language of political science, rational choice) approach in two ways: (1) if people's view of the political world is symbolically constructed, and if the symbols are manipulated by power brokers for their own ends, there is little point in speaking of a rational process whereby political decisions are made, for cognition is filtered through essentially nonrational lenses; and (2) in the rational action model, there is little, if any, room for emotion to affect perception of reality or the decision to take political action, as it certainly does. In the model of politics I have sketched in this book, the emotional dimension is central.[10]

More than half a century ago, writing in his prison cell, Antonio Gramsci argued that the Italian masses would not be politically converted simply through rational argumentation. Rather, he wrote, among the people "philosophy can only be experienced as a faith." If people's political position were based on rational argumentation, they would be in the psychologically untenable position of changing their mind every time someone better informed and better educated than they put forth an argument superior to theirs.[11]

Rational choice theorists have not been without their critics, including those in political science. Donald Green and Ian Shapiro point out that a substantial diversity of approaches fall under the rational choice label, and a number have recognized the need to supplement the rational choice model with some kind of cultural theory. Green and Shapiro lament, however, that after rational choice theorists admit the key role played by "cultural" factors, they turn away from them. Instead they limit their work to those elements that seem to lend themselves to a rational choice model.[12]

Jon Elster, in addressing the question of political belief, takes rational choice theorists to task for coming up with rational reasons for "decisions that are essentially incapable of rational justification." In his view, in order to understand political belief we have to understand people's "need for meaning." By their nature, people need to find a purpose to the forces that affect them (rather than to recognize the complexity and contingency of the world around them), they need to feel that there is some kind of justice in the world, and, more generally, they need to feel that they understand the world. Having some belief, however baseless, may be better than admitting ignorance.[13]

Although I see a role for rational choice models in political study—in some contexts, for example, game theory can produce refreshing insights—the symbolic nature of politics has to be recognized. This is why I focus in this book on symbols, myth, ritual, the perception of reality, and the construction of identity.

The Role of History in Politics

All political leaders tell a story, and their story is inevitably bound up with an account of history. When one regime replaces another, we typically see a radical revision of history: former heroes become villains, those forgotten or previously vilified become deified, what had previously been portrayed as sordid riots become heroic revolts, events are manufactured, and, most of all, the past is endowed with a new structure.

Political movements that seek change must adopt historico-genic strategies. Just how much freedom political elites, or would-be elites, have to alter history for these ends is a ticklish question. "The past is a scarce resource," argues anthropologist Arjun Appadurai. In this view, elites are not free to come up with any new formulation they like but, rather, must abide by a set of cultural norms that limits the plasticity of history.[14]

This is an important reminder and an important topic for investigation. The norms confining historico-genic strategies, though, constrain choices not only at the societal—in our case Italian—level but also at the more specific level—here the micro-culture of the Italian Communist Party. Occhetto faced a series of taboos restricting what could now be said about the past, and these constraints on the production of history had clear consequences for his ability to produce a new future.

The extent of people's resistance to changing the past is linked to the extent to which that past provides them with their present identity, both personal and social. Insofar as people's view of the past produces a sense of belonging to a larger social grouping—be it national, religious, ethnic, or whatnot—fiddling with this construction of history risks altering their social identity and allegiances: their view of who is "us" and who "them."

John Burrow has put it this way: "What gives history its continuing power is not falsehood, nor for that matter truth, but the sense of continuing identity, expressed in re-enactments by ritual and riot." He goes on to argue that the "enemy of such myths is not truth but individualism, the dissolving of the sense of collective identities and temporal continuities."[15]

But how do people create this sense of a continuous past? How do they manage the past in order to keep a firm identity alive in the present? Until 1989, PCI members had iconic representations of the past that, not coincidentally, bore striking parallels to those of the devotees of the church. A silver hammer and sickle dangled from silver chains around the necks of many comrades, replacing the cross; the party sanctum, the local section, had its walls adorned with pictures of the various saints—Lenin, Togliatti, Gramsci, with a sprinkling of Che Guevara and Ho Chi Minh; and the community was likely to be dotted with various sacred reminders of the past: plaques for fallen partisans, shrines for the victims of "Fascist" violence. Revising the party identity in 1989–91 meant revising these iconic representations of the past: some—such as the pendants and the portraits of Lenin—would have to go, while others would remain untouched, testimony to an ambiguous continuity.

In recent years, historians have been paying increasing attention to the problem of memory, of what people recall about the past, and of how those memories are produced. This problem of memory and history relates directly to my discussion of the relation between people's sense of their own history and their ties to various social collectivities. Here, the classic source is Maurice Halbwachs, who has lately enjoyed something of a renaissance. In Halbwachs's view, "The succession of our remembrances, of even our most personal ones, is always explained by changes occurring in our relationships to various collective milieus." He writes, "Each group immobilizes time in its own way." In this perspective, the greatest resource that the social group has is its ability to produce certain memories.[16]

In producing and nourishing memories that link individuals to political groups, rituals play a powerful role. Curiously, in producing history, rites have a way of canceling or telescoping time. The

individual participating in the rite is flooded with memories of previous occasions on which the rites were performed, engendering a
sacred continuity. Rites thus keep alive certain memories and foster
certain views of the past.[17]

Individualism and the Erosion of Party Allegiances

The Italian Communist Party's relation with its members was sub-
stantially different from that of other major parties in Italy. Party
membership was not, especially for those active in the party, simply
one affiliation among many. Rather, it provided a fundamental personal identity. "Io sono comunista" (I am a Communist) defined the
person's sense of self and his or her relation to others in a basic way.
And indeed, one of the poignant problems posed by the abandonment of the Communist party name was the vacuum produced in
people's mode of personal identification. "Noi donne comuniste"
(We women communists), for example, provided a rich basis for
identity for many female party activists, yet the change of party symbolism left nothing with which to replace it ("we democratic women
of the Left" had no resonance; indeed, it seemed ridiculous).[18]

The PCI had initially followed the classic model of the Leninist
cadre party, in which only an elite of committed fighters for
Communism were to be members, and in which devotion to the
Communist cause was to guide all behavior. Yet even with the transformation of the PCI into a mass-membership party at the end of the
war, the legacy of the Leninist model lived on. The statutes called on
all members to be militants, and to recognize that in all spheres of
their social life they would be viewed by others as representatives
of the party. This was, indeed, the basis of the PCI's great strength, a
large membership that identified strongly with the party and that,
through a diversified network of related organizations—from con-
sumer cooperatives to soccer leagues to youth groups to women's
groups—lay at the center of so much social activity.

The redefinition of the PCI must be seen in the context of a gradual erosion of this mode of organization and this type of individual

identification with the party. In the immediate postwar period, local cell and section meetings were heavily attended, and heated discussions about the country's political life animated not only party halls but countless discussions and arguments in smoky cafés, congested courtyards, and cobblestone piazzas throughout the country each afternoon and evening.[19]

The piazzas that once filled each evening with knots of men gesticulating dramatically as they argued over the latest political news are now populated by pigeons and young people strolling through on their way to restaurants and concerts. On weekdays the folks who used to gather nightly in the neighborhood café or the party section are now more likely to be sitting in front of their television sets. On weekends, they can be found by the tens of thousands in their Fiats making their way to second homes in the countryside.

The model of political organization on which the PCI was based was as much undermined by these pervasive forces of social and cultural change as by the blows inflicted by discomfiting international events. Fewer and fewer comrades were willing to spend their Sundays peddling the party newspaper door-to-door. It was becoming more difficult to get the younger members involved in the work required for holding local party feste dell'Unità, and the local feste themselves seemed increasingly quaint. The result was that increased emphasis had to be placed on larger feste, sponsored not at the neighborhood level but by the party's provincial federation.

David Forgacs, reviewing these forces and noting in particular the impact of the growth of private television networks in the 1980s, concluded that the PCI's old form of organization was doomed. The PCI, he wrote, "no longer controls a sufficiently distinct and homogeneous subculture for it to play a significant counter-cultural role or for it to penetrate civil society at local levels with alternative values and goals."[20]

The problem that the party faced was especially severe among the younger generation. The traumatic events of the Second World War, and the consequent hold that its memory had for those who lived through it, deeply affected the PCI. The two million Italians who joined the party in the immediate postwar years gave the party its energy and its leadership for decades. Fortunately for the PCI, just as that cohort began to age, the tumultuous late 1960s—with both student and worker mass protests—brought a new infusion of energy into the party, and a new burnishing of the sacred Communist symbols.

By the 1980s, the huge postwar cohort had begun to die, and the party membership was aging rapidly. Although the 1960s produced a younger cohort of activists and members, these too were passing into middle age. Where previously Italian youth had been seen as particularly predisposed to sympathy for the Left, and hence for PCI recruitment, by the late 1980s this was no longer true. The PCI's image of vigor and youth had given way to one of a party dominated by aging partisans, pensioners, and union bureaucrats.

This does not mean that the split within the party was a generational one. As we have seen, many of the most strident voices against the svolta were those of the young, and indeed in the secessionist Rifondazione comunista the young appear to be as well represented as they are in the PDS. Yet, among the broader population, it is clear that the old symbols that played such an important part in binding people to the PCI—representations of Fascism, of the Resistance, of the October Revolution, and so on—held little of the emotional power for the young that they had for the old.

The Larger Political Nexus

In trying to make sense of the crisis in the Italian Communist Party and the fitful course of its transformation into the PDS, I have focused primarily on internal forces. Occhetto and his allies were pitted against those who opposed the "liquidation" of the party. Both groups did what they could to draw on the wealth of Communist Party symbolism, while redefining both the symbolism and the party's history to suit their tactical needs. Meanwhile, the mass of members coped with the assaults on their identity and struggled to fashion a new identity or devise a way to hold on to the old as best they could.

In concentrating on this dimension, I have underplayed the influence of political forces outside the Communist Party on both the actions of the contending forces of the PCI elite and on the party members and activists themselves. I will not launch here into a full-scale treatment of this larger political framework, nor will I attempt an analysis of party strategy along traditional lines.[21] I will add, however, just a few notes on the impact that outside political forces have had on the transformation of the PCI itself.

I earlier referred to what political commentators in Italy dubbed the "K factor," that is, the association with the Soviet Union and, more generally, world Communism, which stigmatized the PCI and rendered it—in the judgment of most Italians—unsuited to be a partner in national government. Although the PCI gained electoral strength throughout the 1950s and 1960s, growth was slow. In the mid-1970s the pace of electoral success quickened dramatically, and by 1976 both Italian and foreign observers were predicting the imminent entrance of the PCI into the national government and even its likely emergence as the party of the relative majority.

These hopes were soon dashed. In part because of the success of both the DC and the Socialists (PSI) in playing on widespread fears of factor K, in part because of the decreasing allure of the identification with the worldwide Communist movement, and in part because of basic changes in the national economy that undermined the traditional social base of the PCI, the party lost momentum in the following years. In the place of the heady optimism of the mid-1970s came a premonition of inevitable decline. The breathtaking events of 1989 in Eastern and Central Europe only accelerated this growing sense that it would take a major remaking of the party to turn its fortunes around. It was just these considerations that led Occhetto and others of like mind in the party to conclude in 1989 that bold action must be taken.

The symbolism on which the PCI depended derived not only from its own internal activities but from external forces as well. The success of PCI leaders in manipulating symbols depended on the willingness of the party faithful to find them convincing and satisfying, and this clearly was affected by current events and by the way that nonparty media—television most notably—represented them.

But external political forces influenced the internal struggle over PCI identity in a more direct sense as well, for the symbols of identity depended on the willingness of outside forces to recognize them as legitimate and meaningful. Occhetto's efforts to transform the PCI into the PDS demanded not only the support of party members but also the complicity—or perhaps approval is a less loaded term—of non-Communist forces. These outsiders did not have to approve of the new party's program but, if the transformation was to be successful, they did need to certify the claim that the PDS *was* a new party.

By affirming that the Italian Communist Party was no more and that a new party had arisen in its place, the Christian Democrats, Socialists, Republicans, and others helped complete the transformation of political identity that Occhetto had begun. Had these party leaders, and the press, continued to refer to the leaders and members of the "new" party as Communists, as was the convention until 1990, the PDS would have been stillborn. Why these political actors were willing to recognize the PDS in this way, why the daily newspapers did, literally overnight, stop calling "Communists" the political leaders they had for years regularly referred to in this way, would make an intriguing study in itself.

Something similar happened in 1994–95, when the leadership of the Movimento sociale italiano—the party that arose in the postwar period from the surviving leadership of Mussolini's Republic of Salò and identified closely with Fascism—decided to transform their party into a "new" political grouping, the Alleanza nazionale (National Alliance). The ability of Gianfranco Fini and other MSI leaders to alter their party's identity and change its symbolism (Fascist salutes were now out) depended not only—and perhaps not so much—on convincing the MSI membership that this would be a good thing. Rather, the crucial victory for the MSI leader was to win the recognition by outside political leaders of this change of identity. The decision of Silvio Berlusconi to bring the AN into the electoral and, later, governmental alliance that he led, was crucial.

In a further uncanny parallel with the PCI-PDS transformation, a splinter group of the old MSI, seeking to lay claim to the old party symbol, ended up in the same court, the Tribunale di Roma, in a custody dispute over the sacred flame that had been the emblem of the MSI.[22] A member of the splinter group showed just how self-conscious the still-proud-to-be-Fascists were about the importance of myth and ritual to their movement. "We live politics," he told a reporter, "as a faith: with our myths, our martyrs. We live for these sacred moments."[23]

Meanwhile, the two main factions to emerge from the ashes of the disgraced Christian Democratic Party, battling over the DC ancestral name of Popular Party and over the symbolism of the DC, likewise fought their battle in the Roman court in 1995. The matter was resolved, at least for a while, when the two factions negotiated a "reciprocal recognition" and agreed that one group could have the name Popular Party and the other could have the old emblem of the DC, a shield marked by a cross.[24]

The French and British Communist Parties

The stigma of tarnished symbols weighed heavily on the Communists not only in Italy but elsewhere in Western Europe as well (to say nothing of the situation in the former Soviet bloc countries, which has some tantalizing parallels). What made the Italian Communists stand out in this period of the crumbling of the Communist regimes is not only that they had long been the largest Communist party in Western Europe but that they also remained a major competitor for national power. Although the percentage of the vote garnered by other Communist parties in Western Europe declined during the 1980s, many had already been so small as to be politically insignificant.

In addition to their electoral declines, a number of Communist Parties were also riven by factionalism that led to formal splits. The Spanish Communist Party, a vibrant national force in the 1970s, split at least four ways and was reduced to less than 4 percent of the vote by 1986. The Finnish party, one of the most successful in Europe, likewise split, while the Portuguese Communist Party, competing nationally for power in the 1970s, polled only 7 percent for its presidential candidate in 1986.[25]

The Western European Communist parties dealt with their tarnished symbols in different ways, as can be illustrated by what happened in France and Britain. The French Communist Party is an obvious choice for comparison with the PCI, for the two were the most influential Communist Parties in Western Europe, and both had benefited enormously from their identification with the wartime Resistance. Yet since the Soviet invasion of Czechoslovakia in 1968, the paths of the French and Italian parties had diverged, with the French remaining strident defenders of the Soviet Union and the goal of a Communist society. The British Communist Party offers a different sort of contrast, for it was a much weaker party than either the Italian or French, yet, like the PCI, it ultimately chose to unburden itself of its Communist identity.

The French Communist Party (Parti communiste français, or PCF), previously the strongest force on the Left in France, and a powerful influence in the French union movement, declined dramatically in the 1980s. Enjoying more than a fifth of the parliamentary votes in 1978, its share shrank to less than a tenth by 1986. While the Italian Communist Party was rapidly distancing itself from the Soviet Union in the 1980s, the French party became the most prominent defender of the USSR in Western Europe, supporting the Soviet invasion of Afghanistan in 1980, for example, and backing the military takeover on behalf of the Communist Party in Poland in 1981.[26]

Whereas, by the late 1980s, the PCI had begun to abandon the Leninist democratic centralism that had long defined the party structure, the PCF held onto it. Critics took aim at the party's totalitarian bureaucracy and, in particular, the apparently dictatorial power of party head Georges Marchais. While the PCI backed Italian participation in NATO and stressed the importance of a multiparty parliamentary system, the PCF denounced NATO as a tool of American imperialism and continued to portray itself as the Leninist motor of class struggle and revolution.[27]

In the wake of Gorbachev's swift series of moves to undermine the old system of Soviet power, which ultimately led to the collapse of Soviet Communism in 1991, the PCF became "even more royalist than the king." They stood with the Communist Parties of Greece, Portugal, Spain, and Belgium in holding aloft the flag of Communism after it had been taken down in the Soviet Union. The PCF leaders, like Occhetto's opponents within the PCI, argued that the problems that led to the collapse of Communism in the Soviet Union were not those of Communism but, rather, the product of the imperfect application of Communism.[28] While the PCI was inventing a new history, a new identity, and a new future, Marchais and the PCF were waving their old flag, proclaiming the purity of a faith that had been unfairly besmirched.

The situation in which the British Communist Party found itself as the Communist world began to unravel in 1989 was quite different. The British CP, a tiny party of the faithful, had gradually moved away from the Soviet model of society. Yet, despite its increasingly heterodox interpretation of Marxism, its Communist identity—proudly embodied in its name—proved to be its curse. Party historian and CP member Willie Thompson described the party's situation in 1990: "Being unable to escape its past—and being unable . . . to come to terms with anything but an edited and sanitised version of it—it could not overcome the perception among the public at large that its primary function was to act as an agent of the Soviet government."[29] The fall of the East German Communist regime,

Thompson noted, prompted party members to conclude that "they had dramatically put themselves on the wrong side of history."[30]

Although the party had but a tiny fraction of the PCI's membership, vote, political clout, or social influence, the proposals debated by the British Communist Party in 1989–91 did closely resemble those being hotly discussed within the PCI. While the majority agreed that the party had to transform itself into something else, party traditionalists had a different outlook, as Thompson described: "To them the party was their identity and whatever else happened they wanted to keep it in being, preferably retaining the name 'Communist' in the title." As in Italy, the traditionalists lost, and—perhaps influenced by their Italian compatriots—the majority adopted the new name of Democratic Left.[31]

Occhetto's Departure

In the aftermath of the founding of the PDS, the battle over symbolism went on, albeit with gradually diminishing intensity. The PDS leadership continued to contest any reference to the events of 1990–91 as constituting the dissolution of the Italian Communist Party, preferring the murkiness of transubstantiation to an admission that the birth of the new party required the death of the old. It would take a bit more time before the formerly beloved symbols could be treated more roughly.

One can, indeed, argue that the old party never did die, and one could point again to the continuity of symbolism: virtually all the leaders of the PDS are former leaders of the PCI, the symbolic center of the new party remains that of the old (the national headquarters of the PDS, known as Botteghe Oscure, for the street on which it is found), and throughout the country members of the new party continue to meet on the premises of the old, although popular participation has continued its long-term decline.

In order to determine the impact of the party's transformation on its fortunes, it would be helpful if we could keep all external factors constant. The case of Italian politics in the five years following the formation of the PDS in 1991 is, unfortunately for this hope, a spectacular example of dramatic and fundamental change in all aspects of national party politics. The corruption scandal—dubbed Tangentopoli—that erupted in 1992 and led to the indictment of thousands of politicians and business executives, prompted the precipitous demise of the two parties that had long been central to the political system: the Christian Democrats and the Socialists. The Christian Democratic Party formally disbanded, and a major segment of its leadership—making a show of excluding DC leaders under indictment—formed the Partito popolare italiano (Italian Popular Party, or PPI). This involved no little symbolic alchemy itself, as the PPI had been the name of the party founded in the aftermath of World War I, the first Catholic party in Italy, the progenitor of the DC.

In January 1994 alone, not only was the PPI born out of the discredited DC, and not only was the Alleanza nazionale born in an attempt to remake the identity of the neo-Fascist MSI, but entrepreneur Silvio Berlusconi announced his entry into the political scene, at the head of his new political grouping, Forza Italia. It is doubtful that any major country not recovering from war or revolution had ever experienced such dramatic political change.

Just a few months before the first election with this new cast of parties, held in March 1994, the victory of a PDS-led coalition of the Left was widely predicted. As it turned out, though, the election produced a major defeat for the Left, as the Berlusconi-led coalition (Forza Italia, Alleanza nazionale, and the Northern League—formed in the 1980s by fiery Umberto Bossi and dedicated to greater autonomy of the north from the central state) won what later proved to be a fleeting parliamentary majority.

By some measures, the PDS had not done badly. Indeed, the party was on the upswing, increasing its parliamentary vote from 16.1 percent in 1992 (the first parliamentary election since the PDS was created) to 20.4 percent two years later. When the 6 percent of the vote received by the Rifondazione comunista is added, the parties emerging from the old PCI had held their own in the years spanning the collapse of world Communism, a feat that might be heralded as a great victory in other, more stable political contexts. Meanwhile, in 1994 their old nemeses, the DC (now the PPI) and the Socialists, received just 11 percent and 2 percent of the vote, respectively, a vertiginous collapse that no one could have predicted when the battle for the transformation of the PCI was being waged just a few years before.[32]

Yet, shock and anger about the PDS defeat were so great that party head Achille Occhetto felt compelled to resign. He left the top position of the party he had formed with undisguised bitterness, feeling poorly treated by his colleagues. Indeed, when he announced his resignation, the failure of anyone in the party leadership to issue the obligatory call for him to reconsider his decision bespoke the depths of his disgrace.[33]

The Alchemy of Representation

Some in Italy have argued that the transformation of the PCI into the PDS was merely cosmetic, that "only" the name changed. This view is especially common on the Right, where dependence on the symbolism of the Communist devil is too deeply ingrained to give up easily. The fact is, though, that the change of name and accompanying symbolism produced a radical change in the Italian political world. The demise of both the DC and the PSI was linked not only to Tangentopoli but also to the change in the symbolic world prompted by the demise of the PCI. Elites and others fearful of Communist power had less need for a strong DC or a robust PSI to outvote the party that once seemed poised to undermine the capitalist status quo. The club that the leaders of the two parties had wielded over critics unhappy with their corrupt mode of operation was gone.

The results of the alchemy of representation are there for all to see. The secessionist Rifondazione comunista (not without its own tensions and factionalism) now occupies both the semantic and the symbolic space that previously belonged to the PCI. The old Communists of the PDS are no longer to be considered Communists. The importance of this distinction again came to the fore in June 1995 at a meeting in Rome of the leaders of the various reformist parties. On the agenda was the proposal to allow the admission to the coalition of a group that had just split off from Rifondazione comunista, a group that viewed the RC as too extremist. The party heads at the meeting refused to allow the new group into the coalition so long as they refused to remove the word *Communist* from their name.[34]

The forces on the Right, however, have found the Communist bugbear difficult to renounce in doing battle with a party (now the PDS) that threatens their path to power. In the spring of 1995, when it looked as though a coalition composed primarily of the PDS and a reformist Catholic group headed by Romano Prodi might beat the conservative forces in the upcoming regional elections, Berlusconi fumed, "It's the same old tactic from the time of Lenin and Stalin, employing a useful idiot." After thus dismissing Prodi as simply a front for the PDS, Berlusconi went on to say, "I read the names of the members of the national directorate of the PDS. They are all exponents of the old PCI." He repeatedly warned Italians against the new "Communist threat."[35]

The ability to name is at the center of political power, at the heart of political innovation. It entails not only the creation of new symbols but the redefinition of the old. It means crafting not only a new identity, free from the embarrassment of tarnished symbols, but a new history. Overnight, a million Italian Communists were eliminated, a million post-Communists born. The hotly contested power to name once again revealed its magical ability to change the political world.

notes

one **Naming Names**

1. Accounts of Occhetto's visit to Bolognina are found in Walter Dondi, "Il Pci cambierà nome?" *L'Unità*, November 12, 1989, p. 8; and Walter Dondi, "La 'sorpresa' Occhetto," *L'Unità*, November 14, 1989, Bologna section, p. 1. Accounts of the battles of Lame and Bolognina are found in Ceppellini and Boroli (1981:507).

2. Bourdieu (1991:192). Or, as Harrison (1992:236) puts it, "If ritual symbolism serves to legitimise political authority, the question this begs is how the political authority's control of this symbolism *itself* comes to be accepted as legitimate."

3. Mach (1993:265).

4. This account comes from a funeral attended by anthropologist Cris Shore (1993:40). Similar Italian Communist funerals are discussed in Kertzer (1988).

5. Foucault (1980). Also see Hutton's (1993:6) discussion of Foucault's position on the uses of history.

6. Malinowski (1954:100–101).

7. I refer here to Kertzer (1988).

8. Shore (1993:45) discusses this aspect of PCI mythology.

9. Sears (1993:136, 144).

10. Hutton (1993:3–4).

11. See Mosse (1975). For a good overview of Mosse's position in these matters, see Drescher, Sabean, and Sharlin (1982).

12. Curiously, an article published in the PCI weekly, *Rinascita*, four months before Occhetto's announcement proposed jettisoning the PCI name and replacing it with the name Partito democratico della sinistra. Yet the timing was not quite right, and an accompanying article by a higher PCI official sought to place distance between the party and the proposal. Ironically—given the significance the term *cosa* would soon acquire (see Chapter 4)—the name of the latter article (by Fabio Musi) was "C'è un tempo per ogni cosa" (There is a time for every thing). Michele Salvati and Salvatore Vacca, "Cambiare nome: E se non ora, quando?" *Rinascita*, July 29, 1989, pp. 35–38.

13. *Fattore K*, the K factor, came into Italian political parlance in the 1970s through the writings of political commentator and journalist Alberto Ronchey. The *K* refers to the German word for Communist.

173

14. Salvati (1993:124). See also Weinberg (1995:62) and, on the lack of a credible alliance strategy, Daniels and Bull (1994).
15. For an examination of the PCI factions on the eve of the svolta see Bull (1994) and Weinberg (1995).
16. See Belloni (1992) for an English-language overview of the first months of this fase costituente.
17. The PCI secretary is elected not by the congress but by the Central Committee. It is the members of the Central Committee who are elected by the congress.
18. Daniels and Bull (1994:4).
19. These factors are discussed in Belloni (1992:92–95).

t w o   **Making Communist History**

1. See, for example, the overture to Lévi-Strauss (1964).
2. Girardet (1986). My reference to Durand's work derives from Girardet's (1986:20) discussion as well.
3. Gramsci (1971:125–26). See also Sorel (1950).
4. PCI (1976). The opening essay was written by Renzo Trivelli, "Le ragioni della nostra fiducia per l'avvenire del Paese," pp. 4–8.
5. See PCI (1976).
6. Indeed, for many years following the war, among the most successful PCI-linked publications was the monthly *Calendario del popolo.*
7. Berlinguer (1950:19). Curiel was leader of a Communist-allied partisan youth organization who was killed by Fascist forces in February 1945.
8. The text of this resolution of the Eighth Congress of the Federazione PCI di Milano, held May 7–9, 1954, is found in Istituto milanese (1986:401).
9. Provincia di Bologna (1973).
10. Giovannini (1956:5–8).
11. Berlinguer (1950:15).
12. On the sacrality of central space see Smith (1987).
13. These events are described by Shore (1990:40). In his interviews of middle-aged Communists in Perugia in the 1980s, he found that many referred to these events as decisive in attracting them to the PCI.
14. The following rapid history of the PCI should in no way be considered a general history of the party. It is, by contrast, a review of some of the most symbolically significant episodes in the PCI's history, focusing on the ways in which those episodes have been mythologized and ritualized. There are several general works on the history of the PCI, though all have their limits. Paolo Spriano's five-volume *Storia del Partito comunista italiano* (published in 1967–75) is the most

voluminous but represents a point of view closely linked to the party. Galli (1976) has attempted a single-volume history. More limited periods or topics in the history of the PCI are treated in Tarrow (1967), Blackmer (1968), Mammarella (1976), Amyot (1981), Sassoon (1981), Urban (1986), Hellman (1988), and Weinberg (1995). The literature on the history of the PCI is massive. For excellent bibliographies see Serfaty and Gray (1980:233–44) and De Grand (1989:174–75).

15. The PSI was founded under the name Partito dei lavoratori italiani and was renamed Partito socialista italiano three years later. For an English-language history of the PSI see De Grand (1989).

16. From the May 8, 1920, issue of *Ordine nuovo*, quoted in Galli (1976:37).

17. PCI (1969a:35; 1971:12). There was certainly time for them to sing both!

18. Quoted in Galli (1976:47).

19. On this point see Blackmer (1968:9) and Shore (1990:148).

20. Urban (1986:94, 139).

21. Ibid., 125, 140–41.

22. Lajolo (1975:15–16).

23. Urban (1986:108–9, 150).

24. Quoted in Gruppi and Daniele (1971:27–28).

25. Togliatti's position was first publicly expressed on his return to Italy in 1944 in a speech at Salerno, and thereafter the move away from revolution and to an electoral mass-party strategy became known as the *svolta di Salerno* (the Salerno turning point). Togliatti's reasons for advocating this course, and the influence that Stalin's policies had on his decision, remain matters of historical controversy. Note that the PCI leadership was also very much aware of the disaster unfolding in Greece at the time (1944–49), with the Greek Communists opting for armed struggle. On this point see, e.g., the remarks of Mauro Scoccimarro (in Istituto milanese 1986:167) at the Congress of the PCI Federation of Milan, held in October 1945. For more detail on the svolta di Salerno see Lepre (1964).

26. The PCI counted 1,770,000 members by the time of its fifth congress in December 1945 (Sassoon 1981:24).

27. This account is based on Galli (1976:291–92).

28. For a discussion of the asymmetrical relations between the PCI and the church, and of how working-class Italians coped with the conflict, see Kertzer (1980).

29. With the partial exception of 1976–79, when, following the success of the PCI in the 1976 parliamentary election, and in the midst of instability introduced by the terrorist campaign of the Red Brigades, the PCI offered "external" support for a DC-led government (Ginsborg 1990:378–400).

30. See Maitan (1990:30–33) and Amyot (1981:29) on this point.

31. Quoted in Galli (1976:307).
32. Report of Senator Giuseppe Alberganti, Seventh Congress of the Communist Federation of Milan, March 17–19, 1951 (Istituto milanese 1986:276).
33. For instance, Togliatti (1963:5), in his preface to a collection of his introductory reports given to the eighth, ninth, and tenth national party congresses, recalls the context of the eighth congress as follows: "In December 1956, less than a year after the decisions and revelations of the Twentieth Congress of the Communist Party of the USSR, and just a few weeks after the events of Poland and Hungary, it was the moment of one of the most vigorous offensives against us."
34. From Togliatti's report to the Eighth PCI Congress in 1956 (ibid., 20).
35. PCI (1969a:8, 106).
36. Are (1980:33).
37. Berlinguer announced this about-face in 1976. Until that time, anti-NATO slogans and posters had been a regular feature of party festivals and demonstrations.
38. These municipal and regional governments were generally coalitions that included the PSI (Pasquino 1980:94).
39. Are (1983:31). For an analysis of the political importance of the feste dell'Unità see Kertzer (1974).
40. Figures on PCI membership are from Are (1983:tables 10, 14). Proportions of the general population by region are from Campisi, La Bella, and Rabino (1982:table 7).
41. On these developments see Urban (1986:chap. 9).

t h r e e **Saviors and Conspirators**

1. See Gleason (1995).
2. Togliatti (1954:20).
3. Berlinguer (1950:27–29).
4. Togliatti (1954:16).
5. "Direttive della Commissione nazionale d'organizzazione," Rome, November 5, 1956 (PCI 1956:1).
6. Opening report of Giuseppe Alberganti, Ninth Congress of the PCI Federation of Milan (Istituto milanese 1986:420).
7. Report of Luigi Longo (PCI 1954:37, 41, 64).
8. Remarks by Enrico Berlinguer (ibid., 77, 83).
9. Berlinguer (1950:7).
10. Remarks by Umberto Massola (PCI 1954:214).
11. The quote is taken from the Ordine del giorno approvato dal VII congresso nazionale (ibid., 341).

12. There is certainly a study to be done here on the iconography of the PCI and how and why it changed over time. The difficult struggle to get recalcitrant sections to remove Stalin's picture after 1956 would make an interesting story in itself, as would the rise of the particularly unphotogenic Antonio Gramsci as the party's leading visual icon by the late 1960s.

13. Togliatti (1955:36).

14. Sassoon (1981:116).

15. Berlinguer (1950:8, 94).

16. Berlinguer (1970:125).

17. Concluding speech of the 1969 PCI national congress, by Enrico Berlinguer (PCI 1969b:750).

18. In Togliatti (1967:viii).

19. Ibid., 12.

20. Fiori (1970).

21. Togliatti (1967:35).

22. The quote is from ibid., 19.

23. Longo (1969:108).

24. Natta (1971:74).

25. Alessandro Natta (ibid., 70–71) provides a typical account: "It is not by chance that, in Italy, the Communists succeeded in being the most anti-Nazi, anti-Fascist, unitary force; if the Communists were the strength of the partisan units, of the brigades of combatants, of the Groups of Patriotic Action, of the Patriotic Action Squads, and also paid the highest price (there were 575 Garibaldi brigades; of the 256,000 partisan combatants in Italy and abroad, the garibaldini were 153,600; of the 70,930 dead, they were 42,558; of the 30,697 wounded, 18,416 were garibaldini)."

26. A typical example of this discourse is provided by Giancarlo Pajetta (1971:87), a PCI leader venerated for his role in the Resistance: "The Communists were at the vanguard, indeed, they were the force behind the Committees of Liberation (CLN). They sought to transform them from purely party organizations into organizations that were tied in more capillary fashion to the masses, that had representation from the new organizations of youths, women, and workers. But not only did they not cast doubt on the right of the other parties, including the Liberal Party, to belong to the CLN, but indeed they did not even contest their right to a veto."

27. In this context, it is worth stressing that I use the term *myth* here in its anthropological sense of sacred story and not as a negative judgment of historical accuracy per se. In the case of the three elements of the Resistance myth mentioned here, for example, it is clear that there is a much stronger historical basis for

points 1 and 2 than for point 3, but all three involve symbolic reconstructions aimed at producing a powerful narrative with emotional resonance.

28. Gruppi and Daniele (1971:31).

29. Togliatti's remarks quoted here are from "L'intervento di Palmiro Togliatti," Sixth Congress of the PCI Federation of Milan, November 16–18, 1947, found in Istituto milanese (1986:196). Although this kind of vilification of the Allied troops was largely limited to the PCI, the Communists were joined by the Socialists in the effort to depict the anti-Nazi struggle as primarily won through the efforts of the Italian Resistance forces. Hence, for example, the Socialist president of the Province of Bologna commemorated the twenty-eighth anniversary of Bologna's Liberation by recalling that the Allies were able to move "without difficulty" through northern Italy because the partigiani had already driven out the Nazis (Ilario Brini, in Provincia di Bologna 1973:13).

30. From Togliatti's concluding speech to the 1956 national PCI congress (Togliatti 1956a:93). A typical PCI presentation of these events in the later period is provided by a PCI pamphlet on the party during the war, intended for the education of party members (Di Tondo 1971:45–46). It argues that the USSR was forced into the pact for purely defensive reasons. The "double game of the bourgeois democracies," it claims, forced the Soviet Union into taking an action that, "while historically and politically the right one," created a crisis in the Communist Party membership.

31. Urban (1986:180).

32. Speech of Mauro Scoccimarro to the Fifth Congress of the PCI Federation of Milan, reprinted in Istituto milanese (1986:173).

33. Togliatti's speech to the Sixth Congress of the PCI Federation of Milan, reprinted in ibid., 189.

34. "L'ordine del giorno approvato dal VII Congresso Nazionale" (PCI 1954:342).

35. "Grande Scomparso" may be found in the Bologna PCI Federation tribute to Stalin (Federazione bolognese del PCI 1954:20).

36. Quoted (and translated) in Blackmer (1968:29).

37. Berlinguer (1950:93).

38. Remarks of Giuseppe Berti, president of the Associazione Italia–URSS, to the 1951 PCI national congress (PCI 1954:313).

39. Togliatti (1955:32–33).

40. PCI (1960:6–7).

41. One of many examples may be provided here. In a 1956 speech by the head of the PCI for Prato, the secretary noted with pride the new five-year plan announced by the USSR that was to conclude in 1960. This would lead, he proudly proclaimed, "in the space of a few years to the surpassing of the level of productivity of the most advanced capitalist countries." Lest this not be entirely clear,

he parenthetically added: "and hence even that of the United States of America" (Vestri 1956:21).

42. PCI 1969b:65, 67.

43. For example, the theses approved by the Fifteenth National PCI Congress in 1979 (PCI 1979:4–5) include the following: "In the current phase of the historical crisis of capitalism, economic development produces enormous dissipation of natural and human resources . . . and threatens irreversible damage to the natural environment and to the relationship between man and nature." The theses continued, "Within the most highly developed capitalist countries, although a part of the working classes has a relatively high material level of existence, such phenomena as unemployment, social marginalization, violence, criminality, and drug use bring ever-increasing dehumanization. Risks of barbarization hang over them."

44. Speech of Luigi Longo, Eleventh Congress, PCI Federation of Milan, November 22–25, 1962 (Istituto milanese 1986:644).

45. Togliatti's address to the Sixth Congress of the PCI Federation of Milan (ibid., 190–91).

46. Togliatti's address to the Sixth Congress of the PCI Federation of Milan (ibid., 197).

47. Togliatti's address to the Seventh Congress of the PCI Federation of Milan (ibid., 293).

48. Berlinguer (1950:37).

49. Remarks of Mauro Scoccimarro, 1951 national PCI congress (PCI 1954:199).

50. Togliatti's comments on the election are from an interview in L'Unità (April 22, 1948) conducted a month after the elections. On the role of the United States in influencing the 1948 election see Ginsborg (1990:115–16).

51. Speech of Gianfranco Borghini (FGCI 1971:48).

52. Ignazi (1992:152–54).

53. Mieli (1983:iii). See also Green (1994:58).

54. Togliatti's report to the cadres of the PCI Federation of Livorno was given September 15, 1956 (Togliatti 1956a:68–72).

55. The cases of Gramsci and Togliatti differ with respect to their history of complicity with Stalinism. Gramsci was jailed in 1926 and therefore was not directly involved in party activities during the period of Stalin's dictatorship. Later the PCI would make much of an episode that occurred just before Gramsci's arrest, when he sent a letter to the central committee of the Soviet Communist Party, expressing the hope that the internal struggle not be allowed to get out of hand. It was a letter that Togliatti angrily denounced because it did not show the requisite unquestioning loyalty to the ruling group in the struggle against their enemies (Zinoviev, Trotsky, et al.). The letter, however, blamed the crisis primarily

on Stalin's enemies: Zinoviev, Trotsky, and Kamenev. Gramsci's views on Stalin in the remaining years of Gramsci's life, spent in captivity, have been much debated. It is likely that Gramsci did have strong reservations about Stalin, but these were never publicly expressed and had no apparent political effect at the time. What Gramsci might have done had he—like Togliatti—been free is an intriguing but unanswerable question. By contrast with Gramsci, Togliatti was one of Stalin's most vigorous and effective boosters and agents, doing all he could to enforce Stalin's will abroad. There are many biographical studies of Gramsci, including a number in English, although—given their political stance—they typically are eager to do everything possible to make a case for Gramsci's opposition to Stalin. Among the English-language studies see Cammett (1967), Fiori (1970), Boggs (1976), Clark (1977), Joll (1977), Adamson (1980), Sassoon (1987), Germino (1990), and Bellamy and Schecter (1993). The extent of the literature on Gramsci (a good deal of it published in the heyday of his popularity as a theorist and cultural icon in the 1970s) is staggering: Cammett's (1989) bibliography, for example, lists six thousand publications on Gramsci.

56. Theses approved at the Fifteenth National Congress of the PCI (PCI 1979:52).
57. On this point see Urban (1986:238).
58. Togliatti's "Conclusioni alla V Conferenza di organizzazione del Partito comunista italiano (1964)," in Angius (1986:40).
59. Blackmer (1968:181).
60. PCI (1964:62).
61. PCI (1969b:751–52).
62. Theses approved at the Fifteenth National Congress of the PCI (PCI 1979:7).
63. Ibid., 51.

f o u r What's in a Name?

1. PCI (1975:55).
2. The local-level symbolic activities of the PCI sections are the focus of a study by Kertzer (1980). See also Shore (1990) and Li Causi (1993).
3. This point was made by party intellectual Alberto Asor Rosa, who argued that the PCI had played a major role in bringing about national unity: "The powerful effort to make hundreds of thousands of members and millions of sympathizers and voters, from Milan to Naples, from Bologna to Bari, speak the same language probably represents the greatest attempt at mass national cultural unification that Italy has ever known from the time of Unification on." ("Tra passato e futuro," *Rinascita,* June 3, 1990, insert pp. 5–10; quotation on p. 6).
4. For a discussion of the Red Brigades' symbolic warfare see Wagner-Pacifici (1987), Kertzer (1988), Drake (1989), and Catanzaro (1991).

5. Bourdieu (1991:105). In the following discussion, all quotations of Bourdieu are from Bourdieu (1991).

6. Tambiah (1968). See Malinowski's (1954) essay *Magic, Science, and Religion,* originally published in 1925.

7. Foucault (1980). For a fuller discussion see Shapiro (1981).

8. This is a Durkheimian construction echoed in Bourdieu (1991:243).

9. Bourdieu (1991) refers to this as the negotiation of the relational element.

10. Relazione di Achille Occhetto, PCI (1990:22–23).

11. This is argued, for example, by Maitan (1990:98).

12. From document 1, p. 3, of the briefs submitted to the Tribunale di Roma in connection with the civil suit brought by the dissident Rifondazione group against the PDS. For a listing of these documents see the Bibliography.

13. Ibid., p. 6.

14. Nando Dalla Chiesa, "L'orgoglio comunista e il nuovo mondo," *L'Unità,* November 26, 1989, p. 2.

15. Occhetto's comments are found in Fabrizio Rondolino's interview with Occhetto, *L'Unità,* December 3, 1989, p. 9.

16. Mead (1934).

17. Quotations are from Fernandez (1986:11) and Cohen (1977:177–118, 120–121). For a more recent anthropological discussion of the construction of self, which focuses more heavily on the role of individual "agency," see A. P. Cohen (1994).

18. Quoted in Bourdieu (1977:170). The original may be found in Sartre (1971:783).

19. Carlo Pratesi's remarks in "Interventi scritti consegnati alla presidenza del Cc," *L'Unità,* November 11, 1989, p. 16.

20. Ibid, p. 14, remarks by Adriana Ceci.

21. Eugenio Manca, "Questo 1990 in una sezione di Palermo," *L'Unità,* October 26, 1990, supplement pp. 11–12, quotation from p. 11.

22. Franco Arcuti, "Cossutta in assemblea a Perugia: La platea applaude 'Non lasceremo mai questo nome,' " *L'Unità,* September 26, 1990, p. 7.

23. Remarks of Maria Paola Profumo, "Interventi scritti consegnati alla presidenza del Cc," *L'Unità,* November 25, 1989, p. 17.

24. "I verbali del dibattito in Direzione," *L'Unità,* May 11, 1990, p. 4.

25. Letter from Lina Piovana, *L'Unità,* January 9, 1990, p. 14.

26. Raffaele Capitani, "Il partito? Lo chiamerei così: Interviste a volo nelle feste emiliane dell'Unità," *L'Unità,* August 17, 1990, p. 8.

27. Comments by Vincenzo Barbato, secretary of a section composed of automobile workers, "Interventi scritti consegnati alla presidenza del Cc," *L'Unità,* November 25, 1989, p. 19.

28. Letter by Luigi Redaelli, *L'Unità,* February 8, 1990, p. 14.

29. Gavino Angius, "Ma la costituente appartiene anche al no," *L'Unità*, May 23, 1990, p. 2.
30. Livia Turco, "Il dibattito al Comitato centrale," *L'Unità*, November 22, 1989, p. 11. Turco voted with Occhetto in favor of the svolta.
31. Some examples come from the first Central Committee discussion of the proposed name change. Tiziana Arista: "Already three years ago we women felt the need to define ourselves as 'Communist women' because it was only the nexus between the two terms that gave a rationale for our new identity." Ersilia Salvato: "I want to open myself to the new without renouncing my identity as a Communist woman." Grazia Zuffa: "Our experience with the Women's Charter, where we clearly specified our identity as Communist women, teaches us that it was by virtue of clearly indicating our identity that we could have a relationship with other women." *L'Unità*, November 24, 1989, pp. 15, 16, 18.
32. Maria Luisa Boccia, "Il dibattito al Comitato centrale," *L'Unità*, November 24, 1989, p. 13.
33. Gianni Borgna, "Interventi scritti consegnati alla presidenza del Cc," *L'Unità*, November 25, 1989, p. 19.
34. Rino Nanni, "No: questo Partito non è da buttare via," *L'Unità*, February 2, 1990, Bologna section, p. 6.
35. Fassino's phrase was "un nome onorato, di cui non abbiamo certo ragione di vergognarci." Found in "Il dibattito al Comitato centrale," *L'Unità*, November 22, 1989, p. 13.
36. Bourdieu (1977:170–71).
37. Achille Occhetto, "La relazione di Achille Occhetto al Comitato centrale del PCI," *L'Unità*, November 21, 1989, p. 7.
38. One example of such ridicule is found in Federico Coen, "Ma io insisto: Non c'è chiarezza," *L'Unità*, August 19, 1990, p. 2.
39. "Gli interventi dalla tribuna di Rimini," *L'Unità*, February 3, 1991, p. 16.
40. Bourdieu (1991:213).
41. Occhetto's interpretation of the new symbol is to be found in "La dichiarazione di intenti di Occhetto," *L'Unità*, October 11, 1990, pp. 8–9.
42. Document 1, p. 10.
43. Document 2, p. 6.
44. Document 4, p. 5.
45. Document 2, p. 6.
46. Document 3, pp. 1–2.
47. The court "prohibits, for the time being, use by the association in question of the name *Partito comunista Italiano*, use of the initials PCI, and use of the symbol composed of the hammer, sickle, and star on a double flag along with the initials PCI." Document 5, p. 15.

f i v e **Battling over the Past**

The second epigraph to this chapter, from a banner displayed at a demonstration of the Jewish Youth Federation, is taken from an approving description by Luciano Barca in "Gli interventi sulla relazione di Occhetto," *L'Unità*, May 17, 1990, p. 17.

1. Peel (1984:111) poses this question: "How is it that making history, on the plane of social action directed at realising a future, is so closely involved with making history, in the sense of giving accounts of the past?"

2. Scholars, like politicians, need to justify their present concerns by citing holy ancestors.

3. Some of Gramsci's writings on hegemony are collected in Gramsci (1971). See also Fontana (1993) and Simon (1991).

4. Alonso (1992:405).

5. For a discussion of the theory behind this assertion see Kertzer (1988:15–34).

6. Of course iconic representation itself often relies on historical objectification, as in the case of the stars in the American flag (which represent the number of states) or the crucifix.

7. Malinowski (1954); Middleton (1960). See Harrison's (1992) discussion of "ritual as intellectual property," including his discussion of the Lugbara case. The literature on nationalism, history, and symbolic struggle is vast. For anthropological insights see Gellner (1983), Herzfeld (1987, 1991), and Verdery (1991).

8. Alfiero Grandi, "Un vicolo cieco per il Pci, la divisione fondata sui presupposti del sí e del no," *L'Unità*, June 9, 1990, p. 2.

9. Achille Occhetto, "Le conclusioni di Occhetto al 19 Congresso del Pci," *L'Unità*, March 11, 1990, p. 25.

10. Document 3, p. 4.

11. Document 4, p. 16.

12. This phrase is found in the remarks of Gianni Borgna, "Interventi scritti consegnati alla presidenza del Cc," *L'Unità*, November 25, 1989, p. 19.

13. Letter of Luigi Redaelli, *L'Unità*, February 8, 1990, p. 14.

14. Remarks of Luciano Barca, "Gli interventi sulla relazione di Occhetto," *L'Unità*, May 17, 1990, p. 17.

15. Letter by Giovanni Bertolotti, *L'Unità*, January 6, 1990, p. 10.

16. Quoted in Demitry and De Paolis (1993:54).

17. This date is symbolically significant, in that it is one day before the Liberation of Italy from the Nazis—April 25, 1945—a date that remains today a national holiday.

18. Letter by Sergio Crespi, *L'Unità*, November 1, 1990, p. 17.

19. "Gli interventi sulla relazione di Occhetto," *L'Unità*, May 17, 1990, p. 19.

20. Tudor (1972:123–24).
21. Ibid., 125.
22. The attention lavished on the Resistance and the lack of attention paid to popular enthusiasm for the Fascist regime were hallmarks not simply of the PCI but of most Italian political forces. The emphasis given to the Resistance, however, was much greater in the PCI than in any other major party.
23. Luigi Longo, "Report to the Twelfth Congress of the PCI (February 1969)," *PCI Foreign Bulletin* (January–March 1969): 57.
24. Enrico Berlinguer, "The Socialist Movement and the P.C.I.'s March," *Italian Communists*, no. 4 (October–December 1977):120–22.
25. Paolo Bufalini, "Value and Meaning of the October Revolution Today," *Italian Communists*, no. 4 (October–December 1977): 3.
26. "La dichiarazione di intenti di Occhetto," *L'Unità*, October 11, 1990, p. 8.
27. Natalia Ginzburg, "Il nome," *L'Unità*, February 3, 1990, p. 2. What is especially interesting about this impassioned emotional identification with the symbolism of the PCI is that Ginzburg had never joined the party.
28. Comments of Francesco Ghirelli, "Il dibattito al Comitato centrale," *L'Unità*, November 22, 1989, p. 11.
29. Paolo Bufalini, "Il dibattito sulla relazione di Occhetto," *L'Unità*, May 18, 1990, p. 14; Gavino Angius, "Gli interventi sulla relazione di Occhetto," *L'Unità*, July 25, 1990, p. 12.
30. Giancarlo Pajetta, "Gli interventi sulla relazione di Occhetto," *L'Unità*, July 25, 1990, p. 13.
31. Quoted in Sassoon (1981:13). Togliatti's address to the Seventh Congress of the Comintern in 1935 began with these words.
32. Palmiro Togliatti, editorial, *Rinascita*, December 21, 1949, p. 1.
33. "La relazione di Occhetto al Congresso di Rimini," *L'Unità*, February 1, 1991, p. 18. In Chapter 3 I discussed the relationship of Gramsci and Togliatti to Stalin. Party leaders found it easier to make use of Gramsci than to use Togliatti in building this myth of a party always critical toward Stalin. The link between Togliatti and Stalin was hard to deny, given the many years Togliatti spent in Moscow during Fascism, and given Togliatti's role as secretary of the Comintern in the 1930s. Yet any mention of this link was certain to provoke virulent attack within the party. Occhetto apparently learned this lesson when, just three weeks after becoming head of the PCI in 1988 (revealingly, the occasion was his unveiling of a bust of Togliatti), he said that Togliatti was "inevitabilmente corresponsabile" for Stalinism. The bitter reaction to this statement within the party leadership apparently led Occhetto to be wary of making any nonworshipful comments about Togliatti. See Valentini (1990:35–36).

34. Lowenthal (1985:263).
35. Comments of Emmanuele Macaluso, "Il dibattito al Comitato centrale," *L'Unità*, November 22, 1989, p. 13.
36. Paolo Bufalini, " 'Uno scossone al sistema bloccato,' " interview by Eugenio Manca, *L'Unità*, December 16, 1989, p. 9.
37. In Demitry and De Paolis (1993:35).
38. Comments of Italia Carnaroli, "Gli interventi sulla relazione di Occhetto," *L'Unità*, July 25, 1990, p. 11.
39. Again, the Communists were not by any means alone in promulgating such a Manichaean view of the world. For discussion of the Manichaean impulse in American politics in the Cold War years see Gleason (1995).
40. "Motion No. 3: For a Socialist Democracy in Europe," *Italian Communists*, no. 1 (1990): 67.
41. Alfio Gaeta, *L'Unità*, supplement, December 10, 1989, p. 18.
42. Laura Landi, *L'Unità*, supplement, December 10, 1989, p. 4.
43. Another party member also cites Communist martyrs of the past to justify continued Communist identity: "I am against changing the name and the symbol of a party for which many have given their lives." Elisabetta Cosci, "Le mille domande di Livorno," *L'Unità*, October 12, 1990, Firenze-Toscana section, p. 23.
44. Quoted in Demitry and De Paolis (1993:44).
45. Quoted in ibid., 54.
46. PCI (1975:4–5).

s i x Alternative Histories

1. Giuseppe Chiarante, "Giuseppe Chiarante: Comunismo, il nome e non solo," interview by Marco Sappino, *L'Unità*, supplement, November 23, 1990, p. 5.
2. Pier Giorgio Betti, "Le speranze e i dubbi dentro la Fiat," *L'Unità*, November 16, 1989, p. 4.
3. Giorgio Polara, "Il Pci accelera il cambiamento," *L'Unità*, November 14, 1989, p. 3.
4. On the distinction between "model of" and "model for" see Geertz (1973).
5. The name the youths had given to their FGCI section is itself not without significance, for the letter bore the signature of the FGCI circle "Fidel Castro." *L'Unità*, supplement, December 10, 1989, p. 17.
6. Mario Pirani, "I cantori del 'no,'" *L'Unità*, March 10, 1990, p. 6. An interesting and unusual letter along these lines was published in *L'Unità* on January 13, 1990 (Luca Vuotta, p. 14). The author, a party member, after first warning that there must be "no clearance sale of our best political patrimony and patrimony of

ideals," went on to say, "but this should not lead us to overidealize our party or, above all, its past." He then recalled the intimidating way in which those who did not agree with the party line had been treated in the past.

7. "La dichiarazione di intenti di Occhetto," *L'Unità*, October 11, 1990, p. 9.

8. Walter Dondi, "Il PCI cambierà nome? 'Tutto è possibile,'" *L'Unità*, November 12, 1989, p. 8.

9. On such use of history and myth see Sahlins (1981, 1985) and a critique by Obeyesekere (1992).

10. Achille Occhetto, "Un congresso straordinario," interview by Giorgio Polara, *L'Unità*, November 15, 1989.

11. "Il discorso di Occhetto alla Festa dell'Unità," *L'Unità*, September 22, 1991, p. 20. Occhetto had used identical language in his initial presentation of the svolta to the Central Committee of the PCI in November 1989: "And if today we feel the . . . necessity of undertaking the construction of a new history of the world, it is just because we have always affirmed and honored those socialist ideals." "La relazione di Achille Occhetto al Comitato centrale del Pci," *L'Unità*, November 21, 1989, p. 6.

12. The literature on the Resistance is vast. See, e.g., Secchia (1971), Valiani, Bianchi, and Ragionieri (1971), Quazza (1976), Aga-Rossi (1985), and, most important, Pavone (1994). For some English-language sources see Delzell (1961), Ellwood (1985), and Travis (1989).

13. For an example from Bologna see Kertzer (1980:160–62). It should be added, though, that elements of the DC did what they could to discredit the heroic version of the Resistance, attempting to paint the partigiani as cowardly riffraff.

14. Rousso (1991:10, 303).

15. These are taken from Delzell (1961:298).

16. "La relazione di Achille Occhetto al Comitato centrale del Pci," *L'Unità*, November 21, 1989, p. 6.

17. Gino Milli, "La Resistenza non può essere strumentalizzata," *L'Unità*, February 2, 1990, Bologna section, p. 6.

18. Giorgio Battistini, "D'Alema: 'Non si processa il Pci': 'Sulla Resistenza sí e non sono uniti non c'è vergogna del nostro passato,'" *La Repubblica*, September 8, 1990, p. 9.

19. Some idea of these charges can be gleaned from the front-page opinion piece by Lucio Colletti: "Triangolo della Morte, le colpe di Togliatti," *Corriere della sera*, September 6, 1990.

20. I will examine the MSI demonstrations and the PCI counterdemonstrations in Chapter 7.

21. Michele Smargiassi, "Il Pci adesso dice basta: 'Non si può screditare la Resistenza,'" *La Repubblica*, September 6, 1990, p. 12.

22. Vera Schiavazzi, "Il fronte del no contro Fassino, 'ha rotto la tregua nel partito,'" *La Repubblica*, September 8, 1990, p. 9. Luca Fazzo, " 'Su Togliatti ho espresso idee personali,'" *La Repubblica*, September 10, 1990, p. 8.
23. Filippo Falcone, *L'Unità*, December 21, 1990, supplement, p. 2.
24. Achille Occhetto, "Il discorso di Occhetto a Modena: Il segretario del Pci alla Festa dell'Unità," *L'Unità*, September 23, 1990, p. 15.

s e v e n **The Ritual Struggle**

1. For a fuller discussion of my definition of ritual see Kertzer (1988:8–9). For a review of concepts of ritual see Bell (1992).
2. Myerhoff (1984:152).
3. Typical examples of these views may be found in Occhetto's concluding remarks to the Nineteenth Party Congress in 1990, when he admonished: "We cannot remain content with our rites. We would forever remain at the same point" (p. 16). Likewise, following the foundation of the PDS, Occhetto, in trumpeting the importance of the Socialist Party's warm reception of his appearance at their own party congress, said, "It appeared to me to be anything but merely pro forma." ("Consiglio nazionale: La relazione di Occhetto," *L'Unità*, July 5, 1991, p. 29).
4. Gramsci (1971:418).
5. The theoretical perspective employed here is explicated in Kertzer (1988).
6. Rappaport (1975:88) states, "Participation in ritual demarcates a boundary . . . between private and public processes. . . . Participation is the outcome of a dichotomous choice."
7. Rappaport (1975:95) points out that ritual systems naturalize some conventions while in effect branding others unnatural. As a result, "the conventions of other cultural groups are likely to be thought not to be simply different, nor even merely immoral, but abominable." See also Lincoln (1989:9) on the symbolic construction of social borders.
8. Turner (1967:30).
9. Rappaport (1975:89).
10. On Prince Umberto's abortive visit to Milan see Delzell (1961:547).
11. The Polish case is described in Jakubowska (1990). Its implications are further examined in Harrison (1992). See also Kubik (1994).
12. Durkheim (1915). See Kertzer's (1988:61–67) discussion of Durkheim's ritual theory and the role of solidarity. Durkheim's approach was anticipated by Robertson Smith (1889).
13. For a classic statement on the use of rites in producing solidarity without consensus see Fernandez (1965).

14. The salutation is a bit cumbersome to translate. "Cari compagni" means "dear comrades," but here the female-marked "care compagne" is used first, emphasizing that women are being specifically recognized and given grammatical priority.

15. PCI (1969b:124–25), remarks of Gianfranco Borghini to the Twelfth Congress of the PCI.

16. PCI (1955:373).

17. On Berlinguer's China holiday see Urban (1986:338).

18. Giampiero Rasimelli, "Il dibattito al Comitato centrale," *L'Unità*, November 22, 1989, p. 11. On the role of rituals in both hiding and revealing see DaMatta (1977:259).

19. Fabio Inwinkl, "Via dalle lapidi la parola 'fascista,'" *L'Unità*, August 3, 1990, p. 8.

20. Andrea Guermandi, "Non spetta al governo decidere su queste cose," *L'Unità*, August 3, 1990, p. 8.

21. Michele Smagiassi, "Il Pci adesso dice basta: 'Non si può screditare la Resistenza,'" *La Repubblica*, September 6, 1990, p. 12.

22. Eugenio Manca, " 'Non si processa la Resistenza'—Oggi i partigiani protestano sfilando in silenzio," *L'Unità*, September 8, 1990, p. 6.

23. Jenner Meletti, "Il giorno più amaro di Reggio Emilia: La rabbia dei partigiani: 'Giù le mani dalla Resistenza,'" *L'Unità*, September 9, 1990, p. 7.

24. Daniele Mastrogiacomo, "Finiamola col mito della Resistenza," *La Repubblica*, September 9–10, 1990, p. 9.

25. Jenner Meletti, "Migliaia in piazza a Reggio," *L'Unità*, September 9, 1990, Bologna section, p. 1.

26. PCI (1954:10–35).

27. Ibid., 293.

28. Ibid., 240, 272, 316.

29. FGCI (1971:15); remarks of Maria Baronti.

30. FGCI (1971:249).

31. Ritanna Armeni, "PCI: Prossimo venturo," *Rinascita*, March 11, 1990, p. 5.

32. See Kertzer (1992), where I first reported this incident and first examined the Nineteenth PCI Congress.

33. I attended both the Nineteenth and Twentieth Party Congresses; descriptions of these congresses are based, in part, on these direct observations.

34. "Le conclusioni di Occhetto al 19 Congresso del Pci," *L'Unità*, March 11, 1990, p. 26.

35. Luigi Pintor, "Pci, le cose sono due," *Il Manifesto*, March 11, 1990, p. 1.

36. Pietro Spataro, "Resta il dissenso ma tra noi clima diverso," *L'Unità*, March 11, 1990, p. 4.

37. *L'Unità*, September 14, 1990, p. 1.
38. Ibid., p. 4. The "thousand" refers to the ragtag group of soldiers Garibaldi took to Sicily to win the south over to a unified Italian state.
39. Luca Fazzo, "L'orgoglio di Pajetta," *La Repubblica*, September 9, 1990, p. 8.
40. The description of the Pajetta funeral rites is based on Stefano Marroni, "Il funerale di un comunista vero," *La Repubblica*, September 15, 1990, p. 9, and "'Ciao Gian Carlo, non ti scorderemo' Il lungo corteo, l'emozione e gli applausi per l'ultimo saluto," *L'Unità*, September 15, 1990, p. 7.
41. The internal party struggle over the response to the Iraqi situation is discussed by Bull (1994).
42. All quotations from speeches of the congress are taken from transcripts published in *L'Unità*. Descriptions of reactions to the speeches are based on my own observation.
43. Armando Cossutta, "Gli interventi dalla tribuna di Rimini," *L'Unità*, February 3, 1991, p. 16.
44. Ibid.

e i g h t **The Power of Symbols**

1. Foucault (1980); see also discussion in Shapiro (1981).
2. Bourdieu (1990:137–39).
3. Foucault (1980:133).
4. Bloch (1986). See also a discussion of the continuity of political ritual during times of political change in Kertzer (1988).
5. Fernandez (1986:11).
6. Carr (1986:73–74).
7. Ibid., 76, 90–91, 97.
8. Mach (1993:6, 38) discusses this point.
9. Bourdieu (1991:212).
10. For sophisticated rational choice approaches employed by political scientists specializing in the European Left see Katz (1980) and Kitschelt (1994).
11. Gramsci (1971:339).
12. I agree with Green and Shapiro (1994:203) that those championing a rational choice approach need to consider much more systematically the "limits of what rational choice can explain." I also agree with them that instead of attempting to explain all political behavior through rational choice, theorists of this persuasion would be better advised to ask, "How does rationality interact with other facets of human nature and organization to produce the politics that we seek to understand?" (1994:204).

13. Elster (1993:14).
14. Appadurai (1981).
15. Burrow (1981), quoted in Peel (1984:129).
16. Halbwachs (1980:49). The second Halbwachs passage is quoted in Hutton (1993:80). See also Halbwachs (1992). On the social role of memory, also see Fentress and Wickham (1992) and Gillis (1994).
17. Myerhoff (1984:306).
18. On the nature of Communist identity see Shore (1993). By the 1980s the proportion of party members who could be considered activists had shrunk considerably. Perhaps 10 percent of the members took part in section affairs on a weekly or bi-weekly basis, while another 25 percent or so participated in special meetings (such as section congresses). Even those members whose only regular participation was attending annual party feste and voting for PCI candidates, however, often had a strong identification with the party.
19. These gatherings—whether in section halls, cafés, or piazzas—were overwhelmingly composed of men. The study of women's involvement in politics, and in particular their discussion of political issues in less public settings, has hardly begun.
20. Forgacs (1990:108).
21. For one such analysis see Weinberg (1995). For an excellent general treatment of the changing political party situation in this period see Gilbert (1995).
22. On the transformation of the MSI into the AN see Ignazi (1994). News reports on April 14, 1995 (Televideo #109 from the electronic bulletin board Edicola), tell of the decision of the civil court of Rome prohibiting Rauti and the secessionists from using the old MSI symbol, which, according to the court, was the property of the new AN.
23. Claudio Marsilio, quoted in Stefano Di Michele, "I 'fascisti doc' di Rauti all'assalto di An," *L'Unità,* April 2, 1995, p. 6.
24. On this court case see Televideo #110, April 3, 1995. Notice of the settlement is found in Televideo #112, June 24, 1995.
25. Bell and Criddle (1994:228–29).
26. Courtois and Peschanski (1988).
27. Bell and Criddle (1994:1). See also Morris (1994).
28. Bell and Criddle (1994:4–5). The quotation is also from this source.
29. Thompson (1992:9). On the crisis of the British CP in these years see also Callaghan (1993).
30. Thompson (1992:204–5).
31. Ibid., 205–17.
32. For 1994 election results and their analysis see Diamanti and Mannheimer (1994), Mannheimer (1994), and Allum (1994).

33. For accounts of Occhetto's resignation see the Italian daily newspapers of June 14, 1994. For Occhetto's own view of events see Occhetto (1994).
34. I owe this account to Arturo Parisi, who was present at the meeting, held on June 20, 1995.
35. These quotations are taken from Televideo #109 (April 14, 1995) and Televideo #106 (April 10, 1995).

bibliography

The following abbreviations are used in this book to refer to documentation of the civil suit brought by the "Partito comunista italiano" (the group that was to become known as the Rifondazione comunista) against the Partito democratico della sinistra, in the Tribunale di Roma.

document 1: Brief submitted by the Partito comunista italiano, February 8, 1991.

document 2: Brief submitted by the Partito democratico della sinistra, March 4, 1991.

document 3: Brief submitted by the Partito comunista italiano, March 22, 1991.

document 4: Brief submitted by the Partito democratico della sinistra, April 10, 1991, combined with notes submitted by the Partito democratico della sinistra following oral arguments on April 15, 1995.

document 5: Findings of the court, April 26, 1995.

Adamson, Walter L. 1980. *Hegemony and Revolution: A Study of Antonio Gramsci's Political and Cultural Theory.* Berkeley: University of California Press.

Aga-Rossi, Elena. 1985. *Italia nella sconfitta.* Naples: Edizioni Scientifiche Italiane.

Allum, Percy. 1994. "Il mezzogiorno." In *Milano a Roma: Guida all'Italia elettorale del 1994,* ed. Ilvo Diamanti and Renato Mannheimer, pp. 109–16. Rome: Donzelli.

Alonso, Ana. 1992. "Gender, Power, and Historical Memory: Discourse of Serrano Resistance." In *Feminists Theorize the Political,* ed. Judith Butler and Joan W. Scott, pp. 404–25. New York: Routledge.

Amyot, Grant. 1981. *The Italian Communist Party: The Crisis of the Popular Front Strategy.* New York: St. Martin's.

Angius, Gavino, ed. 1986. *Essere comunisti: Il ruolo del Pci nella società italiana.* Rome: Editori Riuniti.

Appadurai, Arjun. 1981. "The Past as a Scarce Resource." *Man* 16:201–19.

Are, Giuseppe. 1980. *Radiografia di un partito.* Milan: Rizzoli.

———. 1983. "Il PCI come organismo politico." In *Il PCI allo specchio,* ed. Renato Mieli, pp. 7–47. Milan: Rizzoli.

Armeni, Ritanna, and Vichi De Marchi. 1991. "Comunisti nel 2000." In *"Chiamateci compagni": Cronache della Rifondazione comunista*, ed. Ritanna Armeni and Vichi De Marchi, pp. 7–27. Rome: Edizioni Associate.

Bell, Catherine. 1992. *Ritual Theory, Ritual Practice*. New York: Oxford University Press.

Bell, D. S., and Byron Criddle. 1994. *The French Communist Party in the Fifth Republic*. Oxford: Clarendon.

Bellamy, Richard, and Darrow Schecter. 1993. *Gramsci and the Italian State*. Manchester: Manchester University Press.

Belloni, Frank. 1992. "The Italian Communist Party: Towards Dissolution and the Unknown." In *Italian Politics*, ed. Robert Leonardi and Fausto Anderlini, vol. 6, pp. 83–103. London: Pinter.

Berlinguer, Enrico. 1950. *I compiti della gioventù: Rapporto presentato al dodicesimo Congresso Nazionale della FGCI (Livorno, 29 marzo–2 aprile, 1950)*. Rome: Edizioni Gioventù nuova.

————. 1970. "Un partito comunista rinnovato e rafforzato per le esigenze nuove della società italiana." Reprinted in *Essere comunisti: Il ruolo del Pci nella società italiana*, ed. Gavino Angius, pp. 113–25. Rome: Editori Riuniti, 1986.

————. 1977. "The Socialist Movement and the P.C.I.'s March." *Italian Communists*, no. 4 (October–December):120–22.

Blackmer, Donald. 1968. *Unity in Diversity: Italian Communism and the Communist World*. Cambridge: MIT Press.

Bloch, Maurice. 1986. *From Blessing to Violence*. Cambridge: Cambridge University Press.

Boggs, Carl. 1976. *Gramsci's Marxism*. London: Pluto Press.

Bourdieu, Pierre. 1977. *Outline of a Theory of Practice*. Translated by Richard Nice. Cambridge: Cambridge University Press.

————. 1990. *In Other Words*. Translated by Matthew Adamson. Cambridge, England: Polity Press.

————. 1991. *Language and Symbolic Power*. Translated by Gino Raymond and Matthew Adamson. Cambridge: Harvard University Press.

Brini, Ilario. 1973. "Intervento del Presidente della Provincia di Bologna." In *Bologna libera*, ed. Provincia di Bologna, pp. 9–16. Bologna: Provincia di Bologna.

Bufalini, Paolo. 1977. "Value and Meaning of the October Revolution Today." *Italian Communists*, no. 4 (October–December):3–22.

Bull, Martin. 1994. "Social Democracy's Newest Recruit? Conflict and Cohesion in the Italian Democratic Party of the Left." In *Conflict and Cohesion in West European Social Democratic Parties*, ed. David S. Bell and Eric Shaw, pp. 31–49. London: Pinter.

Burrow, John W. 1981. *A Liberal Descent: Victorian Historians and the English Past*. Cambridge: Cambridge University Press.

Callaghan, John. 1993. "Endgame: The Communist Party of Great Britain." In *Western European Communists and the Collapse of Communism*, ed. David S. Bell, pp. 121–38. Oxford: Berg.

Cammett, John M. 1967. *Antonio Gramsci and the Origins of Italian Communism*. Stanford: Stanford University Press.

———. 1989. *Bibliografia gramsciana*. Rome: Fondazione Istituto Gramsci.

Campisi, Domenico, Agostino La Bella, and Giovanni Rabino. 1982. *Migration and Settlement*, vol. 17, *Italy*. Laxenburg, Austria: International Institute for Applied Systems Analysis.

Carr, David. 1986. *Time, Narrative, and History*. Bloomington: Indiana University Press.

Catanzaro, Raimondo, ed. 1991. *The Red Brigades and Left-Wing Terrorism in Italy*. London: Pinter.

Ceppellini, Vincenzo, and Paolo Boroli, eds. 1991. *Storia d'Italia*. Novara: De Agostini.

Clark, Martin. 1977. *Antonio Gramsci and the Revolution That Failed*. New Haven: Yale University Press.

Cohen, Abner. 1977. "Symbolic Action and the Structure of the Self." In *Symbols and Sentiments*, ed. Ioan Lewis, pp. 117–28. London: Academic Press.

Cohen, Anthony P. 1994. *Self Consciousness: An Alternative Anthropology of Identity*. London: Routledge.

Courtois, Stéphanie, and Denis Peschanski. 1988. "From Decline to Marginalization: The PCF breaks with French society." In *Communist Parties in Western Europe: Decline or Adaptation?*, ed. Michael Waller and Meindert Fennema, pp. 47–68. New York: Blackwell.

DaMatta, Roberto. 1977. "Constraint and License: A Preliminary Study of Two Brazilian National Rituals." In *Secular Ritual*, ed. Sally F. Moore and Barbara G. Myerhoff, pp. 244–64. Amsterdam: Van Gorcum.

Daniels, Philip, and Martin J. Bull. 1994. "Voluntary Euthanasia: From the Italian Communist Party to the Democratic Party of the Left." In *West European Communist Parties after the Revolutions of 1989*, ed. Martin J. Bull and Paul Heywood, pp. 1–30. New York: St. Martin's.

De Grand, Alexander. 1989. *The Italian Left in the Twentieth Century*. Bloomington: Indiana University Press.

Delzell, Charles. 1961. *Mussolini's Enemies: The Italian Anti-Fascist Resistance*. Princeton: Princeton University Press.

Demitry, Francesco, and Gabriella De Paolis. *Compagno Occhetto, che fare? Critiche e domande degli italiani nelle lettere al segretario del PDS*. Genoa: Marietti.

Diamanti, Ilvo, and Renato Mannheimer. 1994. "Introduzione." In *Milano a Roma: Guida all'Italia elettorale del 1994,* ed. Ilvo Diamanti and Renato Mannheimer, pp. vii–xxii. Rome: Donzelli.

Di Tondo, Franco. 1972. *Il partito dalle leggi eccezionali del fascismo alla seconda guerra mondiale.* Rome: PCI.

Drake, Richard. 1989. *The Revolutionary Mystique and Terrorism in Contemporary Italy.* Bloomington: Indiana University Press.

Drescher, Seymour, David Sabean, and Allan Sharlin. 1982. "Introduction: George Mosse and Political Symbolism." In *Political Symbolism in Modern Europe,* ed. Seymour Drescher, David Sabean, and Allan Sharlin, pp. 1–15. New Brunswick, N.J.: Transaction.

Durkheim, Emile. 1915. *The Elementary Forms of the Religious Life.* Translated by Joseph Swain. Glencoe: Free Press.

Ellwood, David. 1985. *Italy, 1943–1945.* Leicester: Leicester University Press.

Elster, Jon. 1993. *Political Psychology.* Cambridge: Cambridge University Press.

Federazione Bolognese del PCI. 1954. *Dal VII all'VIII Congresso.* Bologna: Edizioni la lotta.

Federazione giovanile comunista italiano (FGCI). 1971. *XIX Congresso nazionale della Federazione giovanile comunista italiano.* Rome: FGCI.

Fentress, James, and Chris Wickham. 1992. *Social Memory.* Oxford: Blackwell.

Fernandez, James. 1965. "Symbolic Consensus in a Fang Reformative Cult." *American Anthropologist* 67:902–29.

———. 1986. *Persuasions and Performances: The Play of Tropes in Culture.* Bloomington: Indiana University Press.

Fiori, Giuseppe. 1970. *Antonio Gramsci: Life of a Revolutionary.* London: New Left Press.

Fontana, Benedetto. 1993. *Hegemony and Power.* Minneapolis: University of Minnesota Press.

Forgacs, David. 1990. "The Italian Communist Party and Culture." In *Culture and Conflict in Postwar Italy,* ed. Zygmunt G. Baranski and Robert Lumley, pp. 97–114. New York: St. Martin's.

Foucault, Michel. 1980. *Power/Knowledge.* Edited and translated by Colin Gordon. New York: Pantheon.

Galli, Giorgio. 1976. *Storia del Partito comunista italiano.* Rev. ed. Milan: Schwarz Editori.

———. 1977. *Storia del Partito comunista italiano.* 2nd ed. Milan: Bompiani.

Geertz, Clifford. 1973. *The Interpretation of Cultures.* New York: Basic Books.

Gellner, Ernest. 1983. *Nations and Nationalism.* Ithaca: Cornell University Press.

Germino, Dante L. 1990. *Antonio Gramsci: Architect of a New Politics.* Baton Rouge: Louisiana State University Press.

Gilbert, Mark. 1995. *The Italian Revolution: The End of Politics, Italian Style?* Boulder: Westview.

Gillis, John R., ed. 1994. *Commemorations: The Politics of National Identity.* Princeton: Princeton University Press.

Ginsborg, Paul. 1990. *A History of Contemporary Italy.* London: Penguin.

Giovannini, Roberto. 1956. "Intervento." In *Lotte e prospettive dei comunisti pratesi,* ed. Partito comunista italiano. Florence: P.C.I. Zona di Prato.

Girardet, Raoul. 1986. *Mythes et mythologies politiques.* Paris: Editions du Seuil.

Gleason, Abbott. 1995. *Totalitarianism.* New York: Oxford University Press.

Gramsci, Antonio. 1971. *Selections from the Prison Notebooks.* London: Lawrence and Wishart.

Green, Barbara B. 1994. *The Dynamics of Russian Politics.* Westport, Conn.: Praeger.

Green, Donald P., and Ian Shapiro. 1994. *Pathologies of Rational Choice Theory: A Critique of Applications in Political Science.* New Haven: Yale University Press.

Gruppi, Luciano, and Aldo Daniele. 1971. *Le grandi scelte nella storia del Partito comunista italiano.* Rome: PCI.

Halbwachs, Maurice. 1980. *The Collective Memory.* Translated by Francis J. Ditter, Jr., and Vida Ditter. New York: Harper and Row.

———. 1992. *On Collective Memory.* Translated and edited by Lewis A. Coser. Chicago: University of Chicago Press.

Harrison, Simon. 1992. "Ritual as Intellectual Property." *Man* 27:225–44.

Hellman, Stephen. 1988. *Italian Communism in Transition: The Rise and Fall of the Historic Compromise in Turin, 1975–1980.* New York: Oxford University Press.

Herzfeld, Michael. 1987. *Anthropology Through the Looking-Glass.* Cambridge: Cambridge University Press.

———. 1991. *A Place in History.* Princeton: Princeton University Press.

Hutton, Patrick H. 1993. *History as an Art of Memory.* Hanover, N.H.: University Press of New England.

Ignazi, Piero. 1992. *Dal Pci al Pds.* Bologna: Il Mulino.

———. 1994. *Postfascisti? Dal Movimento sociale italiano ad Alleanza nazionale.* Bologna: Il Mulino.

Istituto milanese per la storia della Resistenza. 1986. *I congressi dei comunisti milanesi, 1921–1983.* 2 vols. Milan: Franco Angeli.

Italian Communists. 1990. "Motion No. 3: For a Socialist Democracy in Europe." *Italian Communists,* no. 1:66–86.

Jakubowska, Longina. 1990. "Political Drama in Poland: The Use of National Symbols." *Anthropology Today* 6, no. 4:10–13.

Joll, James. 1977. *Antonio Gramsci*. New York: Viking.

Katz, Richard S. 1980. *A Theory of Parties and Electoral Systems*. Baltimore: Johns Hopkins University Press.

Kertzer, David I. 1974. "The Communist Festa in Italy." *Anthropological Quarterly* 47:374–89.

———. 1980. *Comrades and Christians: Religion and Political Struggle in Communist Italy*. Cambridge: Cambridge University Press. New ed., Prospect Heights, Ill.: Waveland Press, 1990.

———. 1988. *Ritual, Politics, and Power*. New Haven: Yale University Press.

———. 1992. "The Nineteenth Congress of the PCI: The Role of Symbolism in the Communist Crisis." In *Italian Politics*, ed. Roberto Leonardi and Fausto Anderlini, vol. 6, pp. 69–82. London: Pinter.

Kitschelt, Herbert. 1994. *The Transformation of European Social Democracy*. Cambridge: Cambridge University Press.

Kubik, Jan. 1994. *The Power of Symbols Against the Symbols of Power*. University Park: Pennsylvania State University Press.

Lajolo, Davide. 1975. *Finestre aperte a Botteghe Oscure*. Milan: Rizzoli.

Lazar, Marc. 1994. "I progressisti." In *Milano a Roma: Guida all'Italia elettorale del 1994*, ed. Ilvo Diamanti and Renato Mannheimer, pp. 73–84. Rome: Donzelli.

Lepre, Aurelio. 1964. *La svolta di Salerno*. Rome: Editori Riuniti.

Lévi-Strauss, Claude. 1964. *Le cru et le cuit*. Paris: Librairie Plon.

Li Causi, Luciano. 1993. *Il Partito a noi ci ha dato! Antropologia politica di una sezione comunista senese nel dopoguerra*. Siena: Laboratorio EtnoAntropologico.

Lincoln, Bruce. 1989. *Discourse and the Construction of Society: Comparative Studies of Myth, Ritual, and Classification*. New York: Oxford University Press.

Longo, Luigi. 1969. "Dal rapporto al XII Congresso del Pci." Reprinted in *Essere comunisti: Il ruolo del Pci nella società italiana*, ed. Gavino Angius, pp. 90–110. Rome: Editori Riuniti, 1986.

Lowenthal, David. 1985. *The Past Is a Foreign Country*. Cambridge: Cambridge University Press.

Mach, Zdzislaw. 1993. *Symbols, Conflict, and Identity*. Albany: SUNY Press.

Maitan, Livio. 1990. *Al termine di una lunga marcia: Dal Pci al Pds*. Rome: Erre Emme.

Malinowski, Bronislaw. 1954. *Magic, Science, and Religion*. Garden City, N.Y.: Anchor.

Mammarella, Giuseppe. 1976. *Il Partito comunista italiano, 1945–1975*. Florence: Vallecchi.

Mannheimer, Renato. 1994. "Forza Italia." In *Milano a Roma: Guida all'Italia elettorale del 1994*, ed. Ilvo Diamanti and Renato Mannheimer, pp. 29–42. Rome: Donzelli.

Mead, George Herbert. 1934. *Mind, Self, and Society*. Chicago: University of Chicago Press.

Middleton, John. 1960. *Lugbara Religion*. London: Oxford University Press.

Mieli, Renato, ed. 1983. *Il Pci allo specchio*. Milan: Rizzoli.

Morris, Peter. 1994. "The French Communist Party and the End of Communism." In *West European Communist Parties after the Revolutions of 1989*, ed. Martin J. Bull and Paul Heywood, pp. 31–55. New York: St. Martin's.

Mosca, Carla. 1991. "Da Arco al Brancaccio: Come nasce un movimento." In *"Chiamateci compagni": Cronache della Rifondazione comunista*, ed. Ritanna Armeni and Vichi De Marchi, pp. 27–39. Rome: Edizioni Associate.

Mosse, George. 1975. *Nationalization of the Masses*. Ithaca: Cornell University Press.

Myerhoff, Barbara. 1984. "Rites and Signs of Ripening: The Intertwining of Ritual, Time, and Growing Older." In *Age and Anthropological Theory*, ed. David I. Kertzer and Jennie Keith, pp. 305–30. Ithaca: Cornell University Press.

Natta, Alessandro. 1971. "La resistenza e la formazione del 'partito nuovo.'" In *Problemi di storia del Partito comunista italiano*, ed. Istituto Gramsci, pp. 57–83. Rome: Editori Riuniti.

Obeyesekere, Gananath. 1992. *The Apotheosis of Captain Cook*. Princeton: Princeton University Press.

Occhetto, Achille. 1994. *Il sentimento e la ragione*. Milan: Rizzoli.

Pajetta, Giancarlo. 1971. "Dalla liberazione alla repubblica: Le scelte del PCI fino al passaggio all'opposizione." In *Problemi di storia del Partito comunista italiano*, ed. Istituto Gramsci, pp. 85–103. Rome: Editori Riuniti.

Partito comunista italiano (PCI). 1954. *VII Congresso del Partito comunista italiano, 3–8 aprile 1951, Resoconto*. Rome: Edizioni di Cultura Sociale.

———. 1955. "Rapporto d'attività." In *IV Conferenza Nazionale del Partito comunista italiano*, pp. 373–96. Rome: Edizioni di Cultura Sociale.

———. 1956. *Documenti politici e direttive del partito (dalla IV Conferenza all XVIII Congresso)*. Rome: PCI.

———. 1960. *Tesi politiche del IX Congresso del Partito comunista italiano*. Rome: PCI.

———. 1964. *Il Partito comunista. Elementi per un corso di studio sulle tesi del X Congresso del P.C.I., III*. Rome: PCI.

———. 1969a. *Pci '70*. Rome: PCI.

————. 1969b. *XII Congresso del Partito comunista italiano: Atti e risoluzioni.* Rome: Editori Riuniti.

————. 1971. *Almanacco Pci 1972.* Rome: PCI.

————. 1975. *Statuto del Partito comunista italiano (approvato al XIV Congresso del Pci, 18–23 marzo 1975).* Rome: PCI.

————. 1976. *Almanacco '77.* Rome: PCI.

————. 1979. *La politica e organizzazione dei comunisti italiani: Le tesi e lo statuto approvati dal XV Congresso nazionale del Pci.* Rome: Editori Riuniti.

————. 1990. *Documenti per il congresso straordinario del Pci.* Vol. 1. Rome: L'Unità.

Pasquino, Gianfranco. 1980. "From Togliatti to the Compromesso Storico: A Party with a Governmental Vocation." In *The Italian Communist Party: Yesterday, Today, and Tomorrow,* ed. Simon Serfaty and Lawrence Gray, pp. 75–108. Westport, Conn.: Greenwood.

Pavone, Claudio. 1994. *Una guerra civile.* 2nd ed. Turin: Bollati Boringhieri.

Peel, J. D. Y. 1984. "Making History: The Past in the Ijesha Present." *Man* 19:111–32.

Popper, Karl. 1961. *The Poverty of Historicism.* 3rd ed. New York: Harper and Row.

Provincia di Bologna. 1973. *Bologna libera: Seduta straordinaria del Consiglio Provinciale per le celebrazioni del 28 Anniversario della Liberazione di Bologna. Provincia e Comprensori* (supplement, July). Bologna: Provincia di Bologna.

Quazza, G. 1976. *Resistenza e storia d'Italia.* Milan: Feltrinelli.

Rappaport, Roy A. 1975. "Liturgy and Lies." *International Yearbook for Sociology of Knowledge and Religion* 10:75–104.

Rousso, Henry. 1991. *The Vichy Syndrome: History and Memory in France since 1944.* Translated by Arthur Goldhammer. Cambridge: Harvard University Press.

Sahlins, Marshall. 1981. *Historical Metaphors and Mythical Realities.* Ann Arbor: University of Michigan Press.

————. 1985. *Islands of History.* Chicago: University of Chicago Press.

Salvati, Michele. 1993. "The Travail of Italian Communism." *New Left Review,* no. 202:117–24.

Sartre, Jean-Paul. 1971. *L'idiot de la famille.* Vol. 1. Paris: Gallimard.

Sassoon, Anne. 1987. *Gramsci's Politics.* 2nd ed. Minneapolis: University of Minnesota Press.

Sassoon, Donald. 1981. *The Strategy of the Italian Communist Party.* London: Pinter.

Sears, David O. 1993. "Symbolic Politics." In *Explorations in Political Psychology*, ed. Shanto Iyengar and William J. McGuire, pp. 113–49. Durham: Duke University Press.

Secchia, Pietro. 1971. *Il Partito comunista italiano e la guerra di Liberazione, 1943–1945*. Milan: La Pietra.

Serfaty, Simon, and Lawrence Gray, eds. 1980. *The Italian Communist Party: Yesterday, Today, and Tomorrow*. Westport, Conn.: Greenwood Press.

Shapiro, Michael J. 1981. *Language and Political Understanding*. New Haven: Yale University Press.

Shore, Cris. 1990. *Italian Communism: The Escape from Leninism*. London: Pluto Press.

———. 1993. "Ethnicity as Revolutionary Strategy: Communist Identity Construction in Italy." In *Inside European Identities*, ed. Sharon Macdonald, pp. 27–53. Providence: Berg.

Simon, Roger. 1991. *Gramsci's Political Thought*. Rev. ed. London: Lawrence and Wishart.

Smith, Jonathan Z. 1987. *To Take Place: Toward Theory in Ritual*. Chicago: University of Chicago Press.

Smith, W. Robertson. 1889. *Lectures on the Religion of the Semites*. Edinburgh: Black.

Sorel, Georges. 1950. *Reflections on Violence*. 1908. Reprint, London: Allen and Unwin.

Spriano, Paolo. 1967–75. *Storia del Partito comunista italiano*. 5 vols. Turin: Einaudi.

Tambiah, Stanley. 1968. "The Magical Power of Words." *Man* 3:175–208.

Tarrow, Sidney. 1967. *Peasant Communism in Southern Italy*. New Haven: Yale University Press.

Thompson, Willie. 1992. *The Good Old Cause: British Communism, 1920–1991*. London: Pluto Press.

Togliatti, Palmiro. 1954. *Per un governo di pace: VII congresso nazionale del Partito comunista italiano, 1951*. Rome: Edizione di cultura sociale.

———. 1955. *La lotta dei comunisti per la libertà, la pace, il socialismo*. 3rd ed. Rome: Edizioni di Cultura Sociale.

———. 1956a. *Per un Congresso di rinnovamento e rafforzamento del Partito comunista*. Rome: PCI.

———. 1956b. "Palmiro Togliatti's Report to the Eighth Congress of the PCI, December 1956." In *The Communist Parties of Italy, France and Spain*, ed. Peter Lange and Maurizio Vannicelli, pp. 33–35. London: Allen and Unwin.

————. 1963. *Nella democrazia e nella pace verso il socialismo: I rapporti e le conclusioni all'VIII, IX e X Congressi del Partito comunista italiano.* Rome: Editori Riuniti.

————. 1967. *Gramsci.* Edited by Ernesto Ragionieri. Rome: Editori Riuniti.

Travis, David. 1989. "Communism and Resistance in Italy, 1943–8." In *Resistance and Revolution in Mediterranean Europe, 1939–1948,* ed. Tony Judt, pp. 80–109. London: Routledge.

Trivelli, Renzo. 1976. "Le ragioni della nostra fiducia per l'avvenire del Paese." In *Almanacco PCI '77,* by Partito comunista italiano, pp. 4–8. Rome: PCI.

Tudor, Henry. 1972. *Political Myth.* New York: Praeger.

Turner, Victor. 1967. *The Forest of Symbols.* Ithaca: Cornell University Press.

Urban, Joan Barth. 1986. *Moscow and the Italian Communist Party.* Ithaca: Cornell University Press.

Valentini, Chiara. 1990. *Il nome e la cosa: Viaggio nel Pci che cambia.* Milan: Feltrinelli.

Valiani, Leo, Gianfranco Bianchi, and Ernesto Ragionieri. 1971. *Azionisti, cattolici e comunisti nella Resistenza.* Milan: Franco Angeli.

Verdery, Katherine. 1991. *National Ideology under Socialism.* Berkeley: University of California Press.

Vestri, Giorgio. 1956. "Intervento." In *Lotte e prospettive dei comunisti pratesi,* ed. Partito comunista italiano. Florence: P.C.I. Zona di Prato.

Wagner-Pacifici, Robin. 1987. *The Moro Morality Play: Terrorism as Social Drama.* Chicago: University of Chicago Press.

Weil, Simone. 1952. *The Need for Roots.* Translated by A. F. Wills. London: Routledge.

Weinberg, Leonard. 1995. *The Transformation of Italian Communism.* New Brunswick: Transaction.

index